The COMPLETE HERB Gardener

Paul Seitz

Sterling Publishing Co., Inc. New York

Disclaimer

There is a widespread belief that because herbs are part of nature, they are harmless. Nothing could be further from the truth. Herbs can be both useful and harmful—even toxic—and the possibility of adverse side effects must keep the user on alert. As the author and publisher have no control over how the reader chooses to utilize the information in this book, they are not responsible for consequences that result from its use. Follow all instructions to the letter for preparation and dosage—provided that the plant is correctly identified—and heed all warnings. Plant life cycles are referenced to the northern hemisphere.

Library of Congress Cataloging-in-Publication Data

Seitz, Paul.
    [Kräutergarten.   English]
    The complete herb gardener / Paul Seitz.
      p.   cm.
    Includes index.
    ISBN 0-8069-3988-5
    1. Herb gardening. 2. Herbs. I. Title.
    SB351.H5S4513   1996
    635'.7—dc20   95-46739
                                      CIP

3 5 7 9 10 8 6 4 2

Published 1996 by Sterling Publishing Company, Inc.
387 Park Avenue South, New York, N.Y. 10016
Originally published and © 1994 by
Franckh-Kosmos Verlags-GmbH & Co., Stuttgart
under the title *Kräutergarten*
English translation © 1996 by Sterling Publishing Co., Inc.
Distributed in Canada by Sterling Publishing
% Canadian Manda Group, One Atlantic Avenue, Suite 105
Toronto, Ontario, Canada M6K 3E7
Distributed in Great Britain and Europe by Cassell PLC
Wellington House, l25 Strand, London WC2R 0BB, England
Distributed in Australia by Capricorn Link (Australia) Pty Ltd.
P.O. Box 6651, Baulkham Hills, Business Centre, NSW 2153, Australia
Printed and bound in Hong Kong
All rights reserved

Sterling ISBN 0-8069-3988-5

Contents

An Overview

Herb Cultivation through History

Herbal science is as old as human history itself. Our ancestors relied on intuition, observation, and experience to use herbs for healing and for flavoring. In Egypt, recipes using herbs for healing purposes date as far back as Dynasty VI. In approximately 2400 B.C., an herb garden was built as part of a school of "medicine" at the Temple Edfu in Upper Egypt.

As early as 750 B.C., gardeners were cultivating sixty-four medicinal herbs in the herb garden of the Babylonian emperor Mardukapaliddina II, including garlic, coriander, caraway, fennel, purslane, dill, mustard seeds, thyme, and hemp.

Fennel was already growing in cloister gardens during the time of Charlemagne, A.D. 742–814.

Hippocrates (ca. 460–ca. 377 B.C.), widely regarded as the "father of medicine," and his students recorded much of what was then known about medical science, extensively covering the use of medicinal herbs for many illnesses.

The Old Testament makes reference to "little herbal gardens," "herb mountains," and "incense hills," indicating a knowledge of herbs as medicine, as incense, and as flavorings.

As the Roman soldiers advanced over the Alps and into northern Europe, they brought with them not only seeds to grow their fruits and vegetables but also seeds for plants used for medicinal purposes and to flavor their food. They did not want to be without the benefits of the healing powers of these plants,

the flavors they added to their food, or the fragrances and incense they provided. This is how many people learned about different varieties of onion, such as garlic and leek, as well as coriander, chervil, watercress, dill, and mint.

After they defeated the Romans during the third and fourth centuries, the peoples of these regions continued to grow and cultivate the plants that the soldiers had left behind, long persuaded of their benefits. The common names of these plants disappeared during the period of Christianization. Latin names replaced them. Eventually, the plants became part of Church ritual. For instance, the use of incense during heathen rituals was not forbidden outright, but was in fact incorpo-

By the ninth century, Benedictine monks considered sage a medicinal herb that possessed magical powers.

fresh plants on hand for the medicine they prepared for the sick. In about A.D. 842, Walahfrid Strabo, the abbot of a Benedictine monastery, wrote *Hortulus*, a verse poem in which he describes the twenty-three different types of herbs, their powers and effectiveness, their individual characteristics, and the care they needed during the course of the growing season.

The Abbess Hildegard von Bingen (1098–1179), widely recognized as a learned scientist of the times, described the healing powers of over 200 different kinds of plants in

rated into celebrations, for instance, "Ascension Day."

The Middle Ages

During the ninth century, the Benedictine monks, whose particular duties included the cultivation of farms and gardens, brought additional beneficial herbs to Europe's more temperate regions (such as sage, mallow, marshmallow, anise, and lovage). Most of these herbs came from the Middle East and the Mediterranean countries. The monks located their gardens as close to the apothecary as possible, ensuring that they always had

*Monks have long been growing mallow (**Malvia sylvestris**).*

Between A.D. *830 and 840, Walahfrid Strabo, a Benedictine monk, wrote* Hortulus, *a poem about the herb garden in his monastery where they grew twenty-three different medicinal herbs, all of which are still in use today.*

her book *Physica*.

Medicine and pharmacology became two distinct entities during the thirteenth century. In 1213, Holy Roman Emperor Frederick II of Hohenstaufen declared both professions to be independent, giving special rights and responsibilities to each. Pharmacists became responsible for the preparation of medicinal remedies. They were to prepare these according to the instructions of a physician. This gave rise to pharmacy gardens, where pharmacists grew the necessary herbs.

The Sixteenth Century to the Present

During the sixteenth and seventeenth centuries, farmers and people in general began to grow herbs for their own use. Church and monastery gardens became the model for rural gardeners. The general population also adapted the Church design, dividing the space with walkways laid out in the shape of the cross, often enhanced by other Christian symbols. The cross-shaped walks protected the garden from evil spirits.

Over the last few years leading to the present day, herbs with medicinal properties have been gaining importance. People from many walks of life show a keen interest in them. Nature lovers and garden enthusiasts want to know more about plants that have healing and aromatic properties, as well as those used for seasoning food.

A Botanical Point of View

In the botanical sense, herbs are short-lived

Lovage grows over several seasons. The leaves above ground die off after the first frost.

Borage is an annual, completing its life cycle in one growing season.

plants that do not produce wooden parts. However, in phytotherapy (plant therapy) and when discussing flavoring agents, the term "herb" includes all types of plants used for medicinal properties or as spices. When they are used for medicinal purposes, the professional term is phytopharmica; when used for flavoring food, the term is simply spices.

Like all other plants, herbs belong to different groups depending on whether they grow for one, two, or several sea-

*Primrose (*Primula veris*).*

Experts estimate that about 20,000 different plants have healing properties or are suitable for use as spices. So far, however, scientists have only researched about 500. About thirty percent of plants from different species of the more than 295 families contain essential oils, making them more or less fragrant.

Protected Plants

In order to ensure biological diversity in our environment, many countries have issued regulations that prohibit the collection and/or harvesting of certain plants in the wild. Governments rank endangered plants in so-called red lists according to the degree to which they are in danger of extinction. Gardeners who plan to add to their collection of medicinal herbs and spices should make sure to consult governmental lists before removing plants from fields or woods.

Nature lovers and garden enthusiasts should look for alternative plants with similar characteristics to ones that are on the endangered list.

sons. Perennials, of course, grow over several seasons.

Herbs that are wild or semiwild are not very demanding and are resistant to environmental influences, diseases, and pests.

Cultivated wild herbs have adapted to their environment and have remained almost totally unchanged. Only a few, such as chamomile, fennel, and marjoram, are more resistant because of systematic crossbreeding.

The leaves of lemon balm contain several essential oils that release a pleasant lemon fragrance when crushed.

Active Substances in Herbs

You can find active substances in plants in several different parts and organs. The chlorophyll-containing leaves are most commonly used for medicinal purposes as well as for seasoning. Generally speaking, they are particularly rich in active substances.

The stem of a plant transports water and nutrients between the roots and the leaves. Aside from nitrates, only very small concentrations of active substances are found in the stem.

The wooden parts and the bark contain substances that serve a plant's metabolic processes, which is why they, too, are important to phytotherapy (for example, the bark of the oak and willow trees).

Roots, as well as rhizomes and tubers, the organs that take up nutrients from the soil, store substances that have medicinal, flavoring, or sweetening properties (for example, parsley roots and rhubarb).

Flowers, rich in pigments, also contain healing substances. Those that give off a strong scent, such as lavender, roses, and lilac, are particularly rich in essential oils.

Fruits have many minerals and vitamins. Wild and cultivated fruits are part of many medicinal products.

Seeds contain a perfect balance of all of the nutritional and active substances necessary for the life of the future plant. Seeds are, therefore, a high-quality food with medicinal value.

Plant Part	Latin Term/ Abbreviation
Whole plant	Herba/Herb.
Leaf, leaves	Folium, Folia/Fol.
Flower, flowers	Flos, Flores/Flor.
Seeds	Semen/Sem.
Fruit, fruits	Fructus/Fruct.
Roots	Radix/Rad.
Rhizome	Rhizoma/Rhiz.
Bulbs	Bulbus/Bulb.
Bark	Cortex/Cort.

Example: *Basilica Herba* = the basil plant; *Sambuci Flos.* = the flowers of the elder bush; *Quercus cortex* = the bark of the oak tree.

Essential oils are highly volatile, intensely fragrant, oil-like substances present in oil glands or scales.

Herbs used for flavoring include those that have oil-like and sulfur-containing substances (responsible for the rather strong taste of radishes, horseradish, some root vegetables, and some of the cabbage family) and those with sulfur-free oils (such as parsley, celery, and carrots).

The effects of essential oils differ widely. For instance, some are stimulating (peppermint), some are soothing (mint or valerian), some have antibacterial properties (thyme), some help heal infections (chamomile), and some stimulate appetite and digestion (spices).

Lavender is rich in essential oils.

The Quality of Herbs

The quality of all plant matter depends on many different but interrelated environmental situations. The strongest influences are climate and soil condition.

Traditionally, we judge the quality of medicinal and nutritional plants solely on the substances that we can detect and analyze. However, this is not sufficient to determine a plant's innate quality for healing. Listing only some of a plant's qualities is not enough for what we need to know.

To determine the overall ecological quality of a medicinal plant, including all its vital activities, a much more inclusive examination is necessary. By making use of methods, such as chromatography, for instance, it is possible to inspect a plant's inner structure through lines, forms, and colors. Using special filters, we can produce such "pictures" from liquid extracts.

Interpreting the pictures, however, requires a great deal of experience

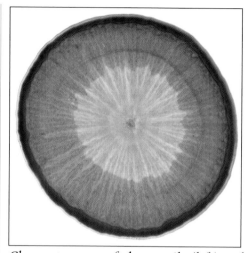
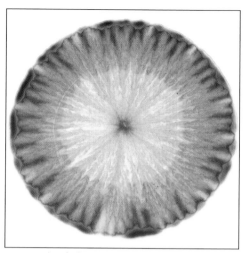

Chromatograms of chamomile (left) and oregano (right) give an overall view of the quality of the plants' color, shape, and lines.

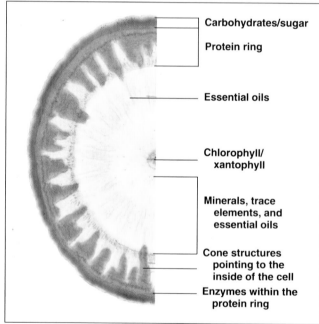

Carbohydrates/sugar

Protein ring

Essential oils

Chlorophyll/xantophyll

Minerals, trace elements, and essential oils

Cone structures pointing to the inside of the cell

Enzymes within the protein ring

Chromatography of chervil (interpretation according to U. Lübke); an increase in the density at the edge determines the amount of carbohydrate/sugar present.
Protein ring: Structures show quality and age. Evenly shaped cones mean that the protein has good quality.
Essential oils: Lines may be difficult to detect.
Enzymes: Markings are within the protein ring.

and is especially useful when used in conjunction with other examination methods.

Of course, we cannot determine the overall quality of a plant without including all relevant information available: data from measurements of partial qualities, an analysis of the substances, and the plant's pH value. Minimum standards of examination have to be met before we can make a final determination. We must also consider other factors, such as storage and transportation (all the way to the consumer).

Using the original method of circular chromatography developed by Dr. Erwin Pfeiffer and Uta and Siegfried Lübke systematically expanded the method of circular chromatography now used to determine the overall quality of nutritional and medicinal plants. This method requires no additional apparatus for quality testing. The photos on page 12 show chromatograms of different herbs, their substances, and behavior.

Fragrant Herbs

In general, all plants give off an aroma. In some cases, the odor is barely noticeable, while in others it is intense. The complex mixture of a plant's fragrance is the result of the interaction of many different (occasionally more than 100) chemical substances. Sometimes the way they mix together produces a distinctive scent, such as the fragrance of violets or of carnations.

Some plants release their fragrance spontaneously, and some release their fragrance only on contact.

A spontaneous release (roses, violets, etc.) occurs when flower buds open. The presence of the fragrance or odor is noticeable but limited, as is the case with fruits. This adaptation has a selective advantage since it assures that the aroma attracts insects for pollination, or that animals will eat the aromatic fruit, seeds, and then disperse the seeds in a natural way.

Plants releasing scent on contact (rosemary, lavender, etc.) release their fragrant substances only after you touch them or crush them. The fragrance in this instance is available throughout a plant's life. Releasing a fragrance on contact also has adaptive advantages in assuring the survival of a particular species, providing protection against pests, and serving as a means of "communication" between different plant species that share the same space.

The violet releases its fragrance spontaneously.

This also has implications in understanding some beneficial partnerships that exist among plants when you use companion planting within your garden (see page 24).

The ability to taste and smell influences the behavior of people and animals in an important way. Many animals have a distinct preference for particular scents. Cats, for example, find the smell of the valerian plant very attractive.

People use pleasant fragrances as "secret" enticements to increase well-being, lift the spirits, and induce purchases in stores and markets.

Medicinal Herbs and Self-medication

Treatment with healing herbs usually does not produce immediate results. Herbs strengthen the body slowly and normalize body functions over time. This is understandable if we remember that most illnesses, too, develop over time. When using herbs medicinally, be careful to protect your body and to minimize any side effects.

The medicinal plants we grow in our herb gardens are very mild. However, side effects are always possible. It is imperative, therefore, to follow all instructions to the letter because every substance has the potential to influence the body negatively, depending on the preparation and the dose.

Use "home-grown" medicine only when the complaint is of the everyday variety. If a condition is chronic or worsens, seek professional medical treatment. Self-made herbal remedies should not be a substitute for proper medical care or for the expertise of

Rosemary releases its fragrance on contact.

a professional pharmacist. You can, however, supplement a course of medical treatment. For instance, an herbal preparation might be helpful in bringing some relief to certain complaints associated with a long-standing condition.

Profiles of individual herbs, including information about their use as natural medicines, begin on page 79.

Avoiding Common Mistakes

Buying Plants

When buying plants, you may not realize that you need to check that you are buying the real thing. This often

Herbs growing in front of the house.

Location

Herb gardens relegated to the farthest corner of the garden may have problems. Because the herbs are not easily visible and are too far away from the house, you may neglect them, resulting in only limited success.

Remedy: Establish the herb garden as close to the house as possible.

Lack of Sun

Herbs planted under trees or in the shade will not grow properly.

Remedy: Most herbs need full sun.

Preparing the Soil

The soil, particularly in new developments, needs help or some herbs will grow very poorly.

Remedy: Treat the area set aside for your garden in a new development with "green" fertilizer to bring it back to life.

leads to disappointment when the quality and quantity of the harvest do not meet expectations. New plants can also spread diseases and pests in your herb garden.

Remedy: Check the quality before purchasing a new plant. Keep the receipt and the identification tag of the plant so that you can exchange your purchase or ask for your money back.

Planting Too Close Together

The area you chose for the garden is too small, and the plants are too close together, or you didn't thin out the young seedlings enough. The plants remain spindly and become more susceptible to pests and diseases.

Remedy: Make sure that plants have enough space. You'll find the requirements for each individual plant in "Plant Profiles," starting on page 79.

Starting Too Early

Some herbs go into the ground too early.

Remedy: Basil, marjoram, cress, dill, purslane, and other herbs are very sensitive to cold. Start them after the weather warms up.

Planting in the Wrong Place

You didn't pay attention to how tall individual herbs will be at maturity, and you didn't check if the plants grouped together are compatible.

Remedy: When planting, consider the future height of the plants and consider how compatible the plants are.

Rotating Crops

You didn't pay enough attention to proper crop rotation when planting annual and biennial herbs. The same is true of perennial herbs propagated by division and cuttings. This often leads to poor growth.

Remedy: Rotate crops properly.

Fertilizing

You used too much fertilizer (particularly nitrogen) before and during the growing season. As a result, your plants grow too fast, become susceptible to diseases, have little fragrance, and are of low quality for medicinal purposes as well as for seasoning.

Remedy: Use organic fertilizer and rely more on mulching.

Watering

Not enough additional watering during periods of drought reduces the crop and its quality at harvest. Soil containing too much acid produces unwanted growth.

Remedy: In most cases, more careful mulching prevents failure.

Pruning

When you fail to cut perennial plants back in the spring, the plants become too scraggly, they spread out too much, and branches begin to droop.

Remedy: Rigorous pruning in the fall prevents unruly growth before the winter sets in. Prune dead twigs in the spring. In addition, pay attention to species-specific needs (see "Plant Profiles," starting on page 79).

Harvesting

Harvesting during unfavorable times and at the wrong time of day reduces the quantity and quality of the herbs.

Remedy: Tips on proper harvesting and processing methods begin on page 58.

An Herb Garden Primer

Planning

When designing an herb garden, you should develop a basic plan that takes into consideration the area available and the needs of the herbs you want to grow, including their sun requirements. Start small, allowing yourself to gain experience.

Planning Tips

• Location: The most important prerequisite for herbs is full sun, since many of them come from regions close to the equator.

Walls always protected the herb gardens in old monasteries. In most cases, the garden received full sun. The surrounding walls and the low beds (see illustration, pages 38–39) kept the different fragrances in the air much longer than if they were in the open.

Gardens that contain herbs primarily used in the kitchen should be as close to the house as possible (provided that there is sufficient sun) so that they are easily available at all times. Stone tiles placed between the plants store the warmth accumulated during the day. You can use the tiles as stepping stones, making weeding and watering that much easier.

• Providing sufficient space for each individual plant is also important. You'll find the needs for each listed in "Plant Profiles," starting on page 79. To avoid a sparse look, you might plant your herbs close together in the beginning, as long as you thin them out later.

• Extreme soil conditions are not good for any plant. You can improve heavy, dense, cold, and wet conditions by adding sand, compost, or bark humus (see page 21). To improve sandy soil, add clay and compost and cover the soil with mulch throughout the season. Mix soil that is too rich in nutrients with sand and peat moss, both of which provide a good chance for plants to survive the winter. This also prevents plants from growing too fast, loosing fragrance in the process.

• The path to and inside the herb garden should be compact and secure so that even in bad weather you can bring herbs into the house without problems. Stones and gravel produce good results.

• Using suitable materials is also important if your garden is to be aesthetically pleasing as well as functional. For walkways, fences, and decorations, choose materials that will complement the environment, such as nat-

Herbs do best when planted in a sunny location.

Herb garden with a stone walk.

ural stones, wood, clay, or ceramics. Wrought iron is also a good choice. Incorporating folk art gives any garden a personal touch.

• Decorative items, such as glass balls mounted on stands, are very popular in some areas. In olden days, people believed that sunlight, reflected in the glass and mirroring the surroundings, would stimulate growth and fertility and protect the garden from evil spirits and marauding birds.

• A whimsical scarecrow is decorative, as is a birdbath, which is also very practical.

• The availability of water is also important. While most herbs are not very demanding, they will suffer during prolonged periods of drought, particularly when the soil is very sandy. Using rainwater collected in a barrel is ideal.

• A garden bench is almost a must in an herb garden. It is the perfect place for spending some leisure time in your garden, enjoying the wonderful fragrances as well as watching birds, bees, butterflies, and the like.

Locating a Garden

When you select the proper location for your garden, you can be sure of long-term success. All herbs used in the kitchen are especially hungry for sun. Provide full sun for your plants, and they will reward you with vigorous growth, fully developed fragrances, and powerful flavors. (Garden cress, chervil, caraway, lovage, horseradish, and sorrel are the exceptions; they will also do well in partial shade.) You can correct problems inherent in your garden soil (see page 21).

A decorative glass ball and a birdbath: combining form with function.

An herb gardens is not just a place to grow plants for medicinal purposes and for the kitchen. When properly designed, it can be a place to simply relax after a hard day's work or on weekends.

Last, but not least, you should always consider the specific requirements and growing habits of each individual plant. A few herbs are really winter-hardy, such as mugwort, sorrel, and wormwood. Others, such as fennel, lavender, oregano, and sage, have gotten used to harsher climates. Since these are perennials, give them extra protection during the winter months. Annuals, such as basil, watercress, and marjoram, are usually fast-growing. Start these indoors (see page 25).

The Soil

Since an herb garden is a permanent fixture within your yard, you have to prepare the soil so that an active or-

Fennel needs additional protection during the winter.

Use a spade to turn over heavy soil in the fall.

Use compost to enrich permanent herb gardens.

ganic life can develop. This is an important prerequisite for the plant's long-term growth.

Testing soil samples for pH value provides information about the amount of phosphoric acid, potassium, and magnesium. Laboratories conducting such tests often provide suggestions in case corrections are necessary. Information about the potassium content and how to prepare the soil prior to planting or seeding is of particular interest to the herb gardener.

The pH value of the soil in herb gardens should be between 5.5 and 6.5, depending on the soil (sandy, sandy/clay, or clay).

Preparing the Soil

Use a cultivator as a hand tool to work additions to the soil (see table on the right) into the upper layer.

Soil Condition	Correction
Heavy, dense, wet, or cold	Add sand, compost, and peat moss
Very light	Add loam and compost, cover with organic mulch throughout the season
Too rich	Reduce by adding sand and do not fertilize

If you prepare the soil for the herb garden during the summer months, there is enough time to grow a soil-building green crop. This is particularly important at the very start, after you have turned over grass or when, after new construction, you have added fill dirt. A green crop might consist of mustard, radishes, or lupine

A personal herb garden.

Till the soil in well-established gardens to a depth of about 12in (30cm) and enrich it with compost.

Some herbs add to the health of the soil. These are savory, borage, dill, watercress, garlic, coriander, peppermint, anise, purslane, and green garlic.

Choosing Plants

When choosing herbs, keep in mind what the primary use will be. For instance, are you growing them for teas, for seasoning, or for their fragrance? For the beginner, it is best to start with well-known herbs, such as peppermint, lemon balm, dill, chives, parsley, and garlic.

You can add other herbs later. Some gardeners have added as many as fifty different herbs, sometimes very rare species.

Most perennial herbs get along well with each other. "Plant Profiles" (starting on page 79) has suggestions for grouping them together according to their height at maturity. You'll also find information on herbs that do not get along together.

Buying Plants

All annual and biennial plants are easy to grow from seed (see page 25). The variety of herb seeds available (including rare ones) has increased tremendously over the last few years.

Even a novice gardener can start perennials from seeds. They are usually started indoors early (see page 25), or (in the case of very robust plants) directly outdoors (see page 26). However, if you are only going to grow one particular herb, it might not be worth the effort to start it indoors, since garden centers, nurseries, and supermarkets offer a wide variety of young plants every spring.

What to Look For When Buying

• Young plants should be healthy and well established. Don't forget to check that the roots are healthy.
• The best choice is a plant that has a well-developed root system.
• Make sure you check type and origin. For instance, German or French tarragon is superior to Russian tarragon. Marjoram, savory, basil, chives, and garden cress are strong plants and usually provide a good harvest.
• Before buying, have the salesperson assure you that the plant you chose is indeed the one you wanted.

You can acquire rare herbal plants by swapping with friends, buying them through special garden catalogs, and, when looking for a very special plant, by checking with the nearest botanical garden.

Starting from Scratch

After you prepare the soil (see page 21), you are ready to begin. You can plant perennial herbs as early as the previous fall, late enough so they don't start growing prematurely (see page 27). When you plant in the fall, it is important to cover them carefully with a layer of rough, organic mulch, 4–6 inches (10–15 cm) thick before the first frost.

In general, however, preparing a garden is part of a gardener's spring ritual, because at that time you seed both the annual and the perennial herbs (see page 26). Planting and laying out walkways go hand in hand.

Placing Plants

Generally speaking, when planting herbs in a so-called border bed, place the tallest herbs in the back; for a bed located more in the middle of the garden, plant the tallest plants in the middle of the bed. In each case, place the medium and low-growing plants in front. If, over time, some plants have not grown to their expected height, perhaps because neighboring plants are interfering, you can always move them to a more appropriate location.

Marigold blooming between leeks in a mulched bed.

Curled parsley serving as a border around a bed of herbs.

Plant annuals and biennials in new locations every year. Some gardeners set aside beds or specific areas within the garden for such crop rotation.

Companion Planting

You can mix herbs used for medicinal purposes and those used strictly in the kitchen. Differing herbs often not only support the healthy growth of all plants but also improve the health of the soil.

Companion planting helps keep the soil healthy.

Beneficial Effects of Spices

Plant	Good Neighbors and Beneficial Effects
Basil	Cucumbers, kohlrabi, salsify, tomatoes, onions
Borage	Strawberries, cucumbers, cabbages, zucchini—defense against cabbage bugs
Chervil	Radishes, lettuce; supposed to defend against snails
Coriander	Strawberries, summer potatoes, cucumbers, all cabbages, beets
Dill	Cucumbers, cabbages, carrots, beets, lettuce
Garden cress	Radishes, horseradish, lettuce
Garlic	Cucumbers, carrots, beets, lettuce, asparagus, tomatoes
Hyssop	Generally beneficial; said to protect against worms
Lavender	Supposed to protect all vegetables against aphids
Leek	All cabbages, carrots, lettuce, celery, tomatoes, onions
Marjoram	Carrots
Mustard	Almost all types of vegetables as long as no cabbage worms are present
Nasturtium	Potatoes, radishes, horseradish, tomatoes, zucchini
Onions	Beans, savory, dill, peas, cucumbers, carrots, lettuce, asparagus
Parsley	Potatoes, cabbages, radishes
Rosemary	Carrots
Sage	Generally beneficial, protects against aphids
Savory	Bush beans, onions; defense against bean lice
Thyme	Generally beneficial; protects against crawling insects

Although there is no research to support the idea, many people believe that fragrant herbs have beneficial effects on the quality and taste of the plants that grow around them. For instance, the flavor of peas, beets, and onions is thought to improve when dill is growing nearby. The taste of fennel and lettuce is thought to improve in the presence of savory. The taste of tomatoes is thought to improve when they are planted with parsley. Radishes seem to taste better in the presence of garden cress, and potatoes seem to improve when coriander, caraway, and peppermint are close by.

Crop rotation is easy with annual herbs, and several perennial herbs have become indispensable in flower gardens. For instance, lavender, sage, hyssop, and thyme are not only beneficial partners for roses and herbaceous plants, they also add a decorative touch.

"Plant Profiles" (starting on page 79) gives information about companion planting, listing plants that benefit from each other and those that do not.

Starting Early

Starting plants early from seeds indoors extends the growing season by several weeks. Use flat containers or dishes for seeding. Sift sandy, humus-containing soil and fill the containers almost to the top. Smooth the soil out and spread the seeds on top. Cover them with a fine substrate or with sand. Only those seeds that need light for germination remain uncovered. Water the soil carefully and cover the box with paper or foil until the seeds germinate. As soon as the small seedlings appear, carefully expose them to the environment by lifting the cover. Don't transplant them until the seedlings show their first leaves.

Transplant the young plants in pots four to five weeks after they develop a strong root system and before you plant them in the garden. However, you must harden all plants before that can take place, which means you must allow them to get used to the outside climate slowly.

Some plants, such as purslane, paprika, basil, and nasturtium, can not tolerate frost and must be indoors as long as there is any danger of frost.

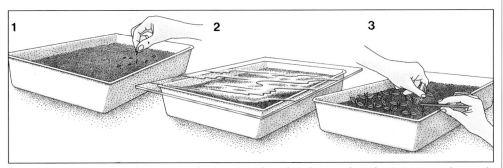

Starting indoors: (1) Cover the sifted soil with a thin layer of seeds. (2) Cover the seeds with sand, carefully spray with water, and cover with window glass. (3) Transplant the seedlings after the first leaves appear.

Growing from seeds: (in the back) a miniature greenhouse; (in front) a box covered with plastic film that you remove after the seeds sprout.

Seedlings growing in a box.

Placing a seed band on the ground.

If a greenhouse isn't available, a miniature greenhouse on a windowsill will do just fine. Such an arrangement is also very practical for propagating with seedlings. A clear plastic top is easy to lift, and you can harden the seedlings in the same container before you plant them outside.

Starting Outside

Sow annual and biennial plants directly in the garden. Sow the seeds in rows. This makes caring for the plants and weeding much easier.

As a general rule, cover the seeds, preferably with sand, with a layer not exceeding two or three times the thickness of the seed. Sow seeds that need light for germination in rows, but don't cover them. The next step is to carefully spray water on the soil. "Plant Profiles" (starting on page 79) gives information on how to handle seeds that require light for germination.

You can buy some herb seeds in so-called seed bands, seed carpets, or seed strips. These usually contain a variety of seeds intended to simplify a gardener's life and improve the rate of success.

In order to get a head start on the season (see page 32) and to be able to harvest fresh greens sooner, you can place perforated polyethylene plastic film or other covering over the seeded garden bed. This allows the soil to warm up

Sowing seeds directly outside:
1. *Prepare the soil properly. Till heavy soil in the fall.*
2. *In the spring, loosen the soil with a cultivator.*
3. *Immediately afterwards, smooth it with a rake.*
4. *When planting in rows, string a cord and draw a groove in the soil.*
5. *Place the seeds in the groove with the required distance between them.*
6. *With the blunt side of a rake, push soil over the seeds and press down.*
7. *Gently water each row.*

much faster, reducing the time for germination. After the last frost, you can remove the covers and save them for use next year.

Be careful! Crawling pests (snails) can hide under the cover, devouring every bit of what is growing underneath. Check regularly and, if necessary, set out traps.

Planting

After properly preparing the soil (see page 21), the next step is to know the space that each plant needs. You'll find this listed in "Plant Profiles" (starting on page 79). You can set the potted seedlings of many herbs (such as paprika, rosemary, thyme, mint, lavender, and tarragon) lower in the soil than they have been in their pots. They are able to grow additional roots on the part of the stem that had been above the soil.

Young plants for sale.

To assure proper root development and growth, firmly press the root ball into the earth with both hands. Roots will then have immediate contact with the soil, minimizing shock to the plant.

Plant perennial herbs early in the fall, but provide protection during the winter. Plant young plants with a well-developed root system outside during April; however, plant frost-sensitive herbs only after the last danger of frost has passed.

Care

Spring

Caring for your garden begins in the spring. Remove winter mulch so that the soil warms up faster. If plants are too close together, this is the time to transplant those that need more space. When transplanting, add to the soil where necessary (see page 22).

Spring cleaning in your herb garden is also the time to prune back your perennials. Cut back all dead branches above ground, and, in the case of shrubs, remove the dead portions of the branches. Cut back into the healthy green part. Other jobs, such as loosening the ground and removing weeds, can be done later, when you get ready to mulch the garden.

Chives start to show reddish purple flowers beginning in June.

Mulching

Organic material, such as bark humus, straw that has begun to rot, and raw compost, works best for mulching. Rake the top portion of the soil. Beginning in April and continuing throughout the summer, add a layer of ¾–1½ in (2–4cm) of mulch on top of the soil when necessary. As protection for the winter, add a layer of 3–4in (8–10cm). Such a covering provides moisture and an even temperature, supports the activity of soil organisms, and assures a steady but slow supply of nutrients. Remove the winter cover in April.

Feeding and Watering

If your soil has a sufficient supply of the main nutrients and is in good condition, your herb garden will have no need for any additional minerals.

Even a small overdose of nitrogen causes rapid, unintended growth, giv-

In a kitchen herb garden, a once-a-year application of well-aged manure is sufficient.

ing other important substances little chance to help the plant. As a general rule, herb gardens only need a healthy layer of compost, ¾in (2cm) thick, or well-aged manure. This supplies all the nutrients the soil needs.

If growth in an older garden begins to slow down, we recommend feeding with hoof shavings, blood meal, or pure, organic, premixed fertilizer. Liquid fertilizers, sometimes made from herbal teas, are fast-acting and very effective.

You can make a liquid fertilizer yourself. Use one shovel of aged manure to 10½qt (10l) of water and mix well. The availability of proper nutrition also depends on proper watering.

Protection

As a rule, chemical treatments are not necessary. Herbs still retain many characteristics of the wild and are very resistant to diseases and pests. You can support this natural ability with appropriate cultivation, the proper location, sufficient space, and proper companion planting.

Other than that, biotechnology determines the degree of protection that your herb garden will have. For instance, if mint, anise, or balm show any sign of rust, or mildew infestation, prune back the plant rigorously, allowing new healthy growth to take place. As a defense against harmful pests, such as cabbage worms and even aphids, use plant covers that allow air, rain, and sun to penetrate but prevent pests from reaching the plant. You can pick off snails and worms by hand, and you can control uninvited night crawlers and other animals by setting traps.

You can protect against unwanted pests and diseases by using methods that are safe for humans and animals and that won't harm your plants. For example, a tea made from horsetail works well against fungus infections. A tea made from stinging nettle is effective against aphids. A tea made from mugwort protects against soil fleas (see page 30). Although these relatively mild biological remedies don't kill pests immediately, they do contribute to the plants' natural resistance. Neither negative residues nor negative side effects are an issue when using natural pesticides.

Protect chives from pests with a vegetable net.

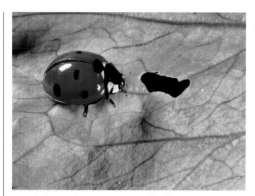

Ladybugs love to eat aphids.

To make a stinging-nettle extract: 1) place part of a fresh plant loosely in a plastic container and fill with water.

Beneficial insects are the natural enemy of pests and have, in a garden managed with natural methods, the best possible living conditions. June bugs and their larvae, the parasite-like ichneumon, and even earworms kill aphids, while predatory mites kill spider mites. You need a wide variety of plants to attract these beneficial insects to the garden. Ichneumon flies lay their eggs into a particular worm. They live on the nectar of the flowers of umbelliferous plants, such as valerian, coriander, caraway, fennel, and dill.

Herbs providing food for beneficial insects: borage, caraway, chervil, common wormwood, coriander, dill, horseradish, lavender, lemon balm, marjoram, medicinal fennel, mugwort, oregano, parsley, peppermint, rosemary, sage, tarragon, thyme, white mustard, and wormwood.

Liquid Manure and Brews

As an herb gardener, you should have a container in which you can keep discarded portions of herbal plants. You will use these to make herbal extracts that will protect your plants from diseases and pests.

Herbal Extracts

As a rule, you need about 2¼lb (1kg) of green-leaf material to make an herbal extract. For instance, cut stinging nettle into 12in (30cm) long pieces and place them in 10½qt (10l) of cold water (rainwater is best). After twelve to twenty-four hours, but no later than three days, the nettle tea is ready to be used as a spray. You can use the extract undiluted to treat aphids (see table, page 32). You can also use it for feeding.

Herbal "Manure"

Herbal extracts begin to ferment in a few days, depending on the temperature. Stir the liquid frequently during the process, which takes ten to thirty-

2) Add several handfuls of stone meal to reduce the odor.

3) The extract is ready in ten to thirty-five days. Use in a 1:10 ratio.

five days. To lessen the odor, add a handful of stone meal every time you stir the pot. Dilute the herbal extract with water in a ratio of 1:10.

Herbal Teas

Herbal teas strengthen plants. Make them by pouring boiling water over fresh leaves (comfrey, dandelion, chamomile, horsetail, or mugwort).

You can also use tea leaves from teas you've made for yourself. Simply pour another cup of warm water over the used leaves and, after a couple of hours, use this tea to water your indoor herbs.

Make a tea that will strengthen your plants from wild horsetail.

Herbal Brew

You can use an herbal brew for several different plant diseases, such as mildew and rust. Make it from fresh or dried herbs. Place them in water for twenty-four hours and then allow them to simmer slowly over low heat for twenty minutes. Pour the mixture through a sieve after it has cooled. You can make a well-known horsetail brew this way. You can make another from rainfern. Steep it, using 10½ quarts (10l) of water for every 10–17 ounces (300–500g) of fresh plant material.

Herb	Use as	Against Disease/Pests
Wild horsetail	Herb tea	Fungus, mildew, rust, mould, celery blight, experiment for cabbage worms
Mugwort (possibly mixed with tomato leaves)	Brew/tea	Fleahopper, cabbage bugs; prevents fungus infection
Rainfern (mixed with horsetail and vermouth)	Tea	Fleahopper, red spider, parasites affecting berry shrubs
Stinging nettle	Cold extract	Aphids
Rhubarb leaves	Tea	Leek moth, black bean lice
Tomato leaves	Cold extract	Cabbage bugs
Fern herbs	Extract	Undiluted, brush on leaves, for aphids; spray during winter, for scale and lice; diluted 10x, for aphids, snails
Pine needles	Dry	Protect against snails
Garlic	Tea	Undiluted against pests
Mix of highly fragrant herbs: dill, lavender, rainfern, garlic, thyme, etc.	Brew tea	Vegetable and fruit flies, ants

Herbs as Biological Protectors

The remedies in the table are the result of general, anecdotal experiences reported by many gardeners. Their effectiveness is not without controversy. However, you can expect that the treatment will strengthen your plants and will at least prevent problems. In any case, it always makes sense to experiment and to carefully observe the results. If nothing else, you will gain new insights and experiences.

Warning: Herbal manure in uncovered containers may be dangerous to children and pets.

Even if they've gone bad, you can use leftover herbs as mulch, or you can add them to compost.

Extending the Growing Season

You can easily extend the growing season for herbs by covering them with foil and vegetable blankets. If the weather is mild, seeding can begin in late winter (February in the northern hemisphere) using any of several methods of covering: plastic film tunnels, perforated

A vegetable blanket covering vegetables.

polyethylene plastic film placed directly over the seeds in the ground, or vegetable blankets. Remember to remove the thick mulch, added for winter protection, prior to covering the beds. This allows the ground to warm up faster. A portable cold frame can also offer protection, producing a wonderful head start on the season. Dill, white mustard, chervil, and several types of cress do very well under a cold frame. As soon as the temperature of the soil is above 43°F (6°C), most herbs will begin to germinate, particularly sorrel, chives, parsley, and several members of the mint family.

You can extend the growing season in the fall in much the same way, often into early winter (December in the northern hemisphere), even if temperatures are already below freezing.

Winterizing

Many favorite perennial herbs are not winter-hardy, such as rosemary, bay leaf, and lemon balm. You have to take

Rosemary needs a bright location and temperatures above freezing.

them out of the ground before the onset of frost. Plant them in a pot and keep them in a cool location inside.

Do not give plants any fertilizer during the dormant period in winter and water them only very sparingly.

Propagating

Sowing

Starting plants from seeds is the method of choice for propagating annual and biennial plants (see page 25).

Cuttings

Only take cuttings from high-quality, healthy mother plants. Do this with a sharp knife, cutting right below a leaf bud. The cutting should be about 2in (5cm) long (see page 34). Allow the cutting surface to dry out, and place the cutting in a container filled with sandy soil.

One of the best methods is the plastic-film covering method. Place wire hoops over the container and cover it with plastic film. Perennial herbs, such as mountain savory, rosemary, wormwood, lavender, tarragon, thyme, mint, and mintlike herbs respond well to this type of propagation.

Division

Dividing older plants that have developed a clump of roots, such as comfrey and sorrel, is a simple and easy method of propagation and is always the method of choice when you only need a few plants. To divide a plant, dig it out of the ground and divide it in half or into quarters. Move the divided plants to a new location at the same time so that you don't exhaust the soil.

Rooted Cuttings

Another method of propagation is rooted cuttings, used, for instance, to propagate mint plants. In this method, you cut a branch in pieces that are approximately 2in (5cm) long. Each piece should already have sprouted some shoots or at least have some buds. You can use this type of propagation outside, but you can also do it in a box, just as with seedlings.

◄

Propagating with seedlings (see page 33): Cut off the seedling with a sharp knife and place it in the soil. Place a miniature plastic-film tent, supported by wire hoops, over the box.

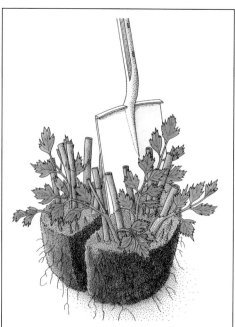

You can cut older plants that have developed a good root ball, with a spade or sharp knife.

Mint plants develop long roots. Separate them into individual sections, making sure that each has at least one bud.

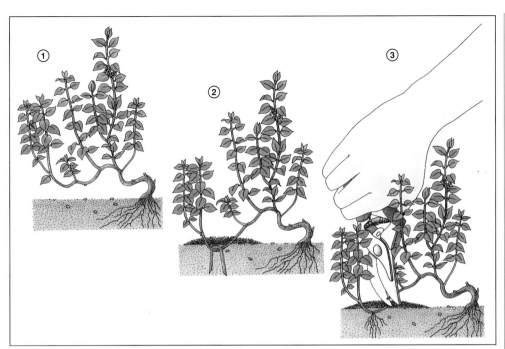

Runners: (1) Choose a stem from a thyme plant. (2) Push it down to the ground and secure it with wire. (3) When roots have developed, separate the new plant.

Runners

You can use so-called runners to propagate a perennial plant, as is often done with thyme. Push branches that have grown sideways down on the ground and hold them in place with a piece of wire that you have bent into a loop. As soon as enough roots have developed, separate the new plant from the mother plant.

Designs

Medicinal plants, herbs for use in the kitchen, and fragrant herbs will do fine when planted among vegetables and flowers in the general garden. However, having their own, separate place makes for a special atmosphere.

A real herb garden should occupy a particular place in the garden. Don't relegate it to a far-off corner. Such an herb garden, created with enthusiasm and ingenuity, will become a focal point within the yard, regardless of whether it is a formal garden or an informal garden allowed to grow naturally and seemingly without effort. You don't have to copy the following suggestions and examples for designing an herb garden as a whole. Take what you like and adjust the suggestions to your particular situation and location.

"Even when the flowers in my large garden are in full bloom, time and again I have observed that my friends linger at the herb garden. I see them reaching out to a plant, tenderly touching a leaf and inhaling the spicy fragrance . . ."

Round herb bed with glass globe ornament.

Strictly Symmetrical Designs

You'll want a strictly symmetrical design if your herb garden is to be part of an existing formal garden. In most cases, however, a gardener decides to go with a geometrical design when the area for the garden is limited and the gardener is trying to make the best possible use of the available space.

The layout of the walkways gives a garden its form. These usually create rectangular beds. Slightly raise the main path and the larger ones on the side to make it easier to keep them

Design with Herbs	Suitable Herbs	Note
Edging	Mints, bee balm, worm-wood, sage, lady's leaf	Contact aroma
Fragrant lawns	Roman chamomile, field thyme	Don't mix plants; plant seedlings; trim often; well suited for walking barefoot in the morning, sunbathing, rest, and relaxation
Seeded directly into the lawn	Native fragrant herbs	Pleasant fragrance after mowing
Fragrant hedges	Lavender, wormwood, cotton lavender	20–30in (50–80cm) high
	Rue, hyssop	12–20in (30–50cm) high
	Germander, thyme	Up to 12in (30 cm) high, frequent cutting
Fragrant walkways	Low mint and oregano, field and lemon thyme, violets, sweet woodruf	Plant robust plants between cracks that have aromatic leaves
	In dry cracks: mountain savory, hyssop, rock carnation	
Fragrant cover	Yarrow, mugwort, thyme, and oregano-like herbs	In full sun; good for difficult locations

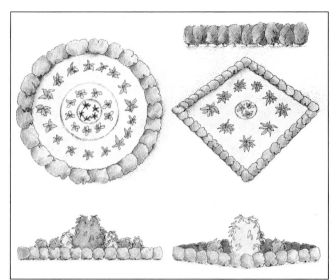

Two symmetrical beds in which you can reach the plants with equal ease from all sides. In the center of the bed are the tallest plants. They grow less and less tall towards the outside edge. A low hedge, such as hyssop, box, or cotton lavender, frames the bed.

Herbs in Beds

Another way of designing your herb garden is to lay out the beds systematically. This is the easiest design to build and also the most practical to take care of. It is also the easiest for the beginner, who, however, should have some experience with planting in rows (such as with vegetables).

clean and to help them dry faster after a rain or after watering. Depending on the overall design, square stone tiles usually work best. They are inexpensive and easy to work with. Individual beds should not be wider than 48in (1.2m), so that they are easy to weed and to harvest. When compared to a garden where several herbs grow in beds (see page 44), here plant only one type of herb in each individual bed. When you plant several in the same bed, pay attention to how tall the herbs are going to be when they mature.

A very attractive way of growing herbs is as part of a patio that is covered with stone tiles. You can remove one or more tiles and plant special, favorite herbs in their place.

Attractive lavender should be part of every herb garden.

A Sunken Garden of Aromatic Herbs

The growing surface of this garden is about 5ft (1.5m) below ground level or surrounded by a wall of equal height. In the latter case, plant the walls surrounding the garden with a fragrant ground cover and low-growing roses (1) or with fragrant shrubs (2), interspersed with individual shrub-like bushes (3), such as elderberry bushes, lilac, or snowball shrub. Scottish climbing roses (4) and holly (5) work well on the west

low border (11) of lavender, wormwood, or germander.

The rest of the beds consist of perennial (12) or annual (13) herbs. Fragrant herbs, such as different types of mint and thyme (14), grow between the stone tiles.

side. You can arrange medium-high shrubs (6) around a bench, while a trellis used for growing clematis, fragrant vine, or climbing roses (7) is shielded by a hedge of clinging vine and summer jasmine (8).

Place a cistern at the center (9). Cover the space in front of the pergola (10) with Roman chamomile or field thyme, around which you can plant a

A small bed of herbs.

When starting an herb garden, rectangular beds work well. The best way to orient the garden is in an east–west direction so that individual beds run in a north–south direction. A so-called kitchen herb garden with annual as well as perennial herbs in rows also works well for companion planting (see page 24) and for the raised method (see page 44).

One-yard (1m) wide beds border the garden on two sides. These are ideal locations for perennial herbs. The north side of the garden may face the house or the orchard. Plant berry shrubs on the east side if there is enough space, about 5ft (1.5m), between them and the herbs. Don't permit high buildings or trees on the west or south side of the herbal garden. This is where the rest of the vegetable and flower garden begins, allowing easy access and as much uninterrupted sunshine as are possible.

Gardens in the Shape of a Cross

The famous herb gardens of the monasteries of the Middle Ages are the basis for this type of layout. These, in turn, took their design from Roman gardens, which themselves were modelled after the early Persian (Islamic) and Egyptian temple gardens. Walls or fences surrounded these ancient gardens. Straight pathways and plants growing in rows separated the beds.

Gardens with walkways laid out in the shape of a cross require a square piece of land. The focal point of the gar-

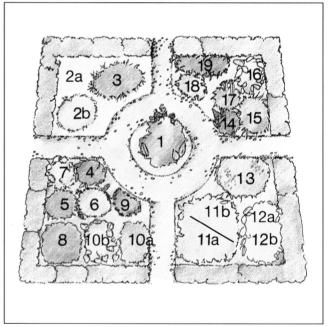

Garden in the shape of a cross: (1) great mullein, elecampane, marshmallow, or hollyhock; (2a) valerian; (2b) dill, tarragon; (3) caraway, coriander; (4) mints; (5) sorrel; (6) wormwood; (7) bee balm; (8) lovage; (9) basil; (10a) marigold; (10b) lemon balm; (11a) thyme; (11b) hyssop; (12a) sage; (12b) lavender; (13) marjoram; (14) pimpernel; (15) oregano, rosemary; (16) fennel, mugwort; (17) borage; (18) parsley; (19) chives. Borders are box, lavender, or cotton lavender.

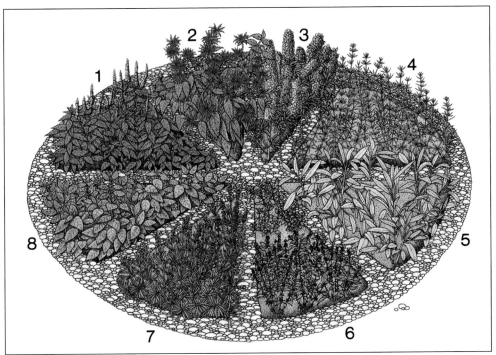

The "fragrant" wheel: (1) apple balm Variegata *(white-green leaves); (2) bee balm; (3) violet; (4) hyssop; (5) sage* Variegata *(white-green leaves); (6) lemon thyme and oregano; (7) lavender; (8) lemon balm* Aurea *(white-green leaves).*

den is usually a combination of taller plants, an attractive sundial in a round bed in the center where the vertical and horizontal walkways cross each other, and/or a small pond or fountain. Gardeners often plant hardy, perennial herbs alongside the walls in beds that are only half as wide as the rest.

Rocks line both sides of the walkways. In more traditional gardens, low-growing plants line the side. The cross-shaped walkways and the symbolic focal point in the center should always be clearly visible.

Wheel-shaped Herbal Gardens

These gardens are round and at least 20 ft (6m) in diameter. The "spokes" of the wheel are walkways that meet in the center, dividing the space into sections. The center, the hub of the wheel, can contain herbs that grow a little taller, such as elecampane, fennel, valerian,

When choosing herbs, pay attention to the plant's mature height.

angelica, or even bay and lemon shrub. Grow other herbs in the space between the "spokes." Plant thyme, hyssop, or mountain savory, trimmed once every year, to keep them low on the outer edge of the wheel.

A garden wheel that features only aromatic herbs (see page 41) is particularly beautiful. Plants that have alternating green and colored leaves (for instance, apple mint, lemon balm, bee balm, violet, sage, lavender, mountain mint, lemon thyme, and oregano) occupy the spaces between the spokes of the wheel.

Irregular Designs

Almost any size property can accommodate an herb garden. Walkways can fit in any landscape. Some might consist of a low ground cover interspersed with flagstone or fieldstone tiles; some accommodate steep terrain by creating a terraced garden. Others might increase growing space by using artificially raised beds.

Plant with the mature height of the plants in mind, so that individual herbs create a wonderful feeling of together-

ness. Over time, these plants will create a real herbal biotope, if the gardener can refrain from interfering with the natural development of the whole.

If the property is large, you might want to design specific areas for different plants.

Plant herbs that need a lot of moisture, such as sorrel or almost any of the mint family, in a spot where drainage isn't ideal. You could also put them next to a pond, where they can spread out unencumbered. Put plants that tolerate partial shade near or under trees and bushes. Place those that need full sun and prefer dry soil along a fence or wall where the soil is sandy and rocky.

Of course, the side of the house with plentiful sun is the ideal place for herbs used in the kitchen. Tiled walkways assure easy access to the garden. The stones can be flat fieldstones, natural stones, irregularly shaped sandstone, or bricks. Other materials worth mentioning are gravel, sand, and tree bark. Grass-covered walkways or those consisting only of compacted dirt also work very well.

No herb garden should be without a birdbath. Colorful glass balls add another wonderful accent to the environ-

A colorful bed of herbs with dill, bee balm, marigold, and others.

Herbs from the mint family love moisture and grow well in marshy soil.

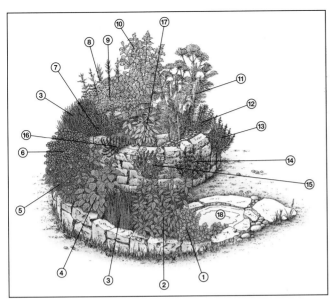

The spiral garden: (1) nasturtium; (2) mints, sorrel; (3) chives, garlic; (4) borage; (5) marigold; (6) parsley, chervil; (7) anise; (8) vermouth; (9) mugwort; (10) lovage; (11) fennel, dill, tarragon; (12) rosemary; (13) savory; (14) hyssop; (15) Jenny stonecrop; (16) thyme; (17) sage; (18) pond.

ment, as does artwork that you have created yourself. Any of the above will give your garden a very special and personal note.

Spiral Herb Gardens

If you only have a limited amount of space, a spiral shape is the design of choice. This type of arrangement accommodates many different plants and their specific needs. Such a garden can have a place for plants that need moisture and love a humid environment, as well as a place for plants that require a minimum of water, all in a relatively small space.

The best location for the garden is in full sun. The garden should be circular and at least 10ft (3m) in diameter. Build a stone mound in the center of the circle, about 20–28in (50–70 cm) high. Drainage on a raised bed is excellent, and this type of bed also stores warmth. Cover the mound with pre-mixed garden soil or with potting soil

A spiral bed of herbs.

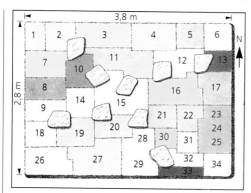

A family herb garden: (1) lovage; (2) vermouth; (3) fennel and tarragon; (4) angelica, mugwort; (5) lavender; (6) rosemary; (7) dill; (8) borage; (9) coriander; (10) sage; (11) apple mint; (12) lemon balm; (13) tall sorrel; (14) radishes; (15) peppermint; (16) grape, wormwood; (17) hyssop; (18) oregano; (19) lemon thyme; (20) thyme; (21) mountain savory; (22) garden savory; (23) chives; (24) border onion; (25) garlic; (26) basil; (27) parsley; (28) marjoram; (29) purslane; (30) white mustard; (31) anise; (32) chervil; (33) nasturtium; (34) garden cress.

mixed with sand. Use fieldstones or other rocks to build the spiral. A damp zone at the side of the mound towards the sun (south in the northern hemisphere) might end in a small pond which should be about 30in (75cm) in diameter. Line it with plastic.

Instead of a pond, you may also use an open barrel or a cistern, buried low enough in the ground so that only the surface of the water is visible.

The water controls the climate of the garden: Strong sunshine evaporates water, maintaining humidity. During night frost, it protects the plants from freezing. Use the pond and its surrounding space for plants that need moisture (in the water: watercress; in the marshy portion: sorrel, plants from the mint family, and goldenrod).

Enrich the soil in the middle and lower sections by adding nutrients from compost. Make sure that you plant herbs that grow taller towards the middle. Place plants that need more shade on the north side, such as chervil, caraway, lovage, and parsley. Place plants of the mint family and tall sorrel where the soil is damp. Mountain savory and Jenny stonecrop grow well in the cracks between the rocks.

Large Herb Beds

In many cases, gardeners prefer a permanent place where they can grow their herbs throughout the year. If well cared for, 130 sq ft (12 sq m) of space will be sufficient for a family of four. A bed measuring 10 × 13ft (3 × 4m) will accommodate thirty different kinds of herbs.

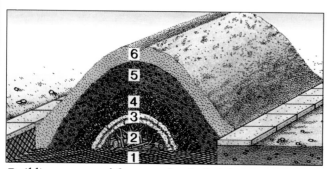

Building a mound for a garden bed: (1) wire as protection against rodents; (2) wood chips, branches, or other rough material; (3) sod; (4) rough compost; (5) semicured compost; (6) garden soil and fieldstones or tiles. Don't forget to make a hollow for watering.

To make caring for the garden and harvesting easier, place stone tiles between groupings of plants.

Raised Garden Beds

Raised beds and those built on a mound work especially well for seniors and for people with disabilities. The borders should be 16–36in (40–90cm) high and built with fieldstones, railroad ties, or round wooden poles. You can add benches facing the sun. Surround the whole bed with a walkway made from fieldstone tiles or similar materials.

Before adding garden soil, you might want to put down an 8–12in (20–30cm) layer of sand or gravel to improve drainage. Plant low-growing herbs that spread rapidly, such as thyme and nasturtium, between cracks or as a border. They will make a wonderful decorative addition when the leaves and flowers begin to spill over the edges.

Layout for planting herbs on a raised bed: (1) borage, cress, chives; (2) tarragon, rosemary, sage; (3) mugwort, lovage, balm, grapes, wormwood; (4) dill, mint family, oregano, hyssop; (5) basil, marjoram, parsley.

Growing Herbs on a Mound

These kinds of bed are less expensive to build than raised beds. They make it easy to use organic kitchen and yard waste.

Build mounded beds in a ditch filled and built up with several different materials. The first layer is either wood chips, branches, or similar materials that decompose. You may also add other rough garden wastes, such as twigs and stems, leaves, sod, and raw compost. Finish this layer by returning the soil you removed when digging the ditch. At this point the overall height of the mound should be about 30–40in (80–100cm). The bed can be as long as you want. A north–south orientation is best because it provides a maximum of sunshine. Make sure that you provide an indentation at the top along the whole length of the bed. This prevents the soil from drying out too rapidly, particularly in the first year. Ideally, the mound will increase the growing surface by about thirty percent.

You can use garden beds built up this way for growing herbs after the first year. In the first year, it is best to plant strong vegetables (tomatoes, cucumbers, zucchini) as an intermediate crop (see page 21). Change to herbs in the fall; better yet, wait until the following spring. Reserve perennial herbs and those that grow taller for the upper rows. Plant annuals and low-growing herbs on the lower rows.

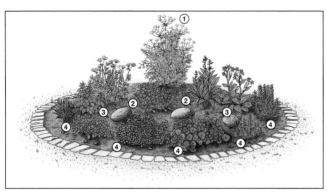

Round raised bed for growing herbs: (1) lovage, fennel; (2) dill, tarragon, chervil, parsley, mint; (3) sage, lavender, borage; (4) chives, basil, marjoram, oregano, nasturtium, thyme, hyssop.

Yellow and orange marigolds add beauty to a raised bed.

The shape of a raised round bed is very special. Built in the right spot, it never looks out of place, even in a regular flower garden. Construct these beds, about 8ft (2.5m) in diameter, in the same way as oblong beds. Here, too, taller plants grow on the upper half.

Arrange plants that grow to medium height and the low-growing plants on the lower level. At ground level, surround the whole bed with fieldstone tiles, to make it easy to care for and to harvest.

As an extra touch, include herbs with distinctive flowers and fragrances: great mullein, marigold, nasturtium, borage, hyssop, thyme, and others from the mint family.

> Raised herb beds also work well when combined with vegetables and flowers.

Alternative Herb Gardens

Gardeners who use alternative methods will encounter no problem when growing herbs. Medicinal herbs and those used for seasoning are resistant to disease and usually don't need supplemental feedings. Well-known alternative methods used in the general vegetable garden are useful in the herb garden as well.

Treating plants with herbal teas and brews (see page 21) strengthens their immune system. Using humus is a key factor in growing herbs alternatively, buttressed by proper mulching methods. If additional nutritional applications are necessary, a great variety of organic fertilizers is available. These will not negatively influence the quality of medicinal herbs, fragrant plants, or herbs used for seasoning food.

Permaculture

Permaculture is a very special system for growing herbs. A spiral walkway, on flat or hilly ground, winds itself to a central point with a fountain or pond. Watercress grows in the area immediately surrounding the source of water. In no particular order, a variety of medicinal herbs, spices, and aromatic plants grows on both sides of the spiral walkway.

Circle Gardening, Findhorn, and Mandala Gardens

Those interested in efficient gardening have found that their plants do better when grown in oval or round beds: leaves are richer in chlorophyll, and most plants are more resistant to diseases.

The circle, the mystical shape of sacred places, is where people used to gather together. The center of the circle represents not only the symbol of eternal power but also the place of "inexhaustible energy" of all that grows and becomes. Every plant, just as every human being and every animal, is the center of its own universe.

Langham uses the circle garden. He grows his herbs in round, so-called crater-beds. An indentation in the center assures a better "connection" to the earth's energy field.

The Findhorn community in the north of Scotland also uses round beds. The model came from old monastery gardens. The community believes that these designs are especially effective "energy fields" beneficial for growing herbs.

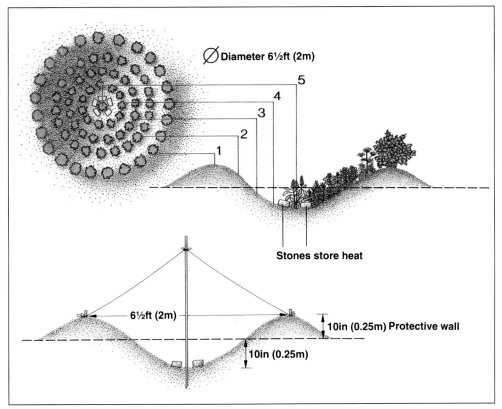

Ø Diameter 6½ft (2m)

Stones store heat

6½ft (2m)

10in (0.25m) Protective wall

10in (0.25m)

Circle gardening suggested planting: (1) Ring (center of wall): lovage, mugwort, worm-wood, tarragon, hyssop, oregano, wormwood, rue. (2) Ring: dill, borage, parsley, cher-vil. (3) Ring: balm, plants from the mint family, oregano, different types of thyme, anise. (4) Ring: basil, savory, marjoram, garlic, chives. (5) Center of crater: plants that are sensitive to cold, like rosemary, sage, or lavender.

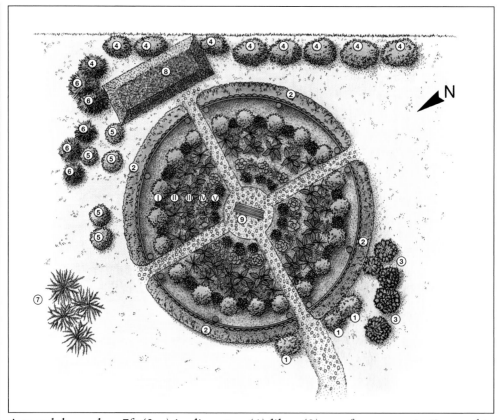

A mandala garden, 7ft (2m) in diameter: (1) lilac; (2) comfrey, as protection and to attract bees, rhubarb; (3) great bindweed; (4) hedgerow maple as protection against wind; (5) elderberry; (6) pine; (7) birch; (8) compost; (9) bench.
Ring I: Berry bushes, between low-growing herbs.
Ring II: Leek, peas, different kinds of onions, beans.
Ring III: Different kinds of cabbage, celery.
Ring IV: Different kinds of salad.
Ring V: Tall medicinal herbs and spices, radishes, beets, parsnip, salsify.

The round beds, designed in the shape of a mandala, are very impressive and economical. The circular shapes inside the mandala, in ancient Indian, Buddhist, and Taoist traditions, have "mystical" connections between all that is alive on earth and the universe as a whole. Density, healing, and growth determine the rhythm of "movement" in a mandala. An "organism" capable of drawing energy to itself is capable of healing itself and of assuring continued growth and development beyond itself. The center of a mandala is always a point of calm and quiet, a place where one can sit down, linger, and relax. Four symmetrical spokes extend from this center, symbolic of the four points of the compass. Each spoke is a walkway that leads to the center.

Fragrant Gardens

The backbone of an aroma garden is the evergreen plant that carries its fragrance in its leaves.

Plants that store their fragrances in the flowers are like special messengers, celebrating different days and periods during the year. In other words, a fragrant garden does not simply exist for practical reasons. Rather, it is a place where carefully selected aromatic plants provide fragrant delights throughout the year.

Gardens that combine both medicinal and seasoning herbs with aromatic plants are practical as well as attractive. This is particularly true when they grow in a garden bed below ground level (see drawing, page 38). The best place for developing the fragrance of an herb is in full sun. Use enough fieldstone tiles (for walkways as well as for decorative purposes), and you will have created an ideal means of storing the heat from the sun that your garden can utilize in small increments in the evening and throughout most of the night.

Aromatic herbs for the garden: rosemary, thyme, lavender, chamomile, muscatel grapes, Roman chamomile, sweet woodruff, angelica, meadowsweet, evening primrose, bee balm, elecampane, herbs from the mint family, curry herb, sage.

Herbs for Cosmetic Uses

In cosmetic physiology, the state of a person's skin, hair, eyelashes, and fingernails is an expression of that person's well-being and proof of a healthy metabolism. Cosmetic preparations for rejuvenation consist not only of substances used externally, such as creams, compresses, facial lotions, facial masks, and diverse preparations for bathing (for recipes see page 74), they also include herbal teas, juices, and herbal extracts for internal intervention, including (always in conjunction with a healthy diet) the use of spices.

An herb garden for natural cosmetics only would be a unique undertaking. Such a garden would be, by design,

Evening primrose gives off a rich fragrance in the evening.

Meadowsweet has a very strong, somewhat sweet fragrance.

This garden contains herbs used for their fragrance as well as for cosmetic purposes, such as creams, hair-coloring preparations, and similar uses.

(1) Witch hazel (Hamamelis virginiana) (2) rugosa rose (Rosa rugos) (3) rosemary (Rosmarinus officinalis) (4) violet (Viola odorata) (5) burdock (Arctium lappa) (6) arnica (Arnica chamissonis) (7) lavender (Lavandula angustifolia) (8) lemon thyme (Thymus × citriodorus) (9) box tree (10) verbena (Verbena officinalis) (11) alyssum (Lobularia maritima) (12) iris (Iris germanica) (13) common heliotrope (Heliotropium arborescens) (14) lemon balm (Melissa officinalis) (15) marigold (Calendula officinalis) (16) gasplant (Dictamus albus) (17) white mustard (Sinapis alba, from seeds) (18) peppermint (Menttha × piperita).

rather small. But that does not mean that a cosmetic garden could not also be very attractive with the proper combination of herbs and other decorative materials. It could be a small, magical, sunny rock garden or a very special garden bed decorated with a glass ball or beautiful birdbath. The advantage of having your own cosmetic herb garden is that the herbs you want to use are always fresh and available when needed.

A cosmetic herbal garden should never be without lady's mantle.

The following herbs should be part of any garden that grows herbs for cosmetic use: *Aloe vera*, chamomile, comfrey, fennel, lady's mantle, lavender, marigold, rosemary, sage, southernwood, violet, and yarrow.

"Plant Profiles" (starting on page 79) also lists the characteristics of herbs used for natural cosmetic preparations.

Herbs for Dyeing Fabrics

The ancient art of dyeing cloth and wool with plant colors has become one of the favorite pastimes for nature lovers today. It is particularly exciting when, just as in olden days, the plants come from your own garden. You can easily grow these between other herbs or bushes, but you an also set aside a special place in your garden for them.

The best colors come from fresh herbs, flowers, tender young leaves, and ripe fruit. Roots and onion skins need to dry after harvesting before you use them.

Harvest the leaves of the yellow-blooming dyer's madder in the summer.

Cornflower in full bloom.

Hops.

The most important plants used for coloring are: dyer's madder, chamomile, mignonette, saffron, broom, elderberry, bedstraw, elecampane, cornflower, hops, goldenrod, meadowsweet (see photo, page 51), and rainfern.

Such a garden can be formal or informal (for a plan see page 35). The choice of herbs is important, so that sufficient food is available from early spring to late fall.

The center of the garden is a beehive or a box that receives full sun and has a source of water.

Plants must include those of the Labiatae and Umbelliferae families. Others are borage, buckwheat, and valerian. Also include a patch with greens that produce early pollen for food. An ornamental red or black currant bush and a lot of comfrey also attract bumblebees. A lilac bush will attract many different butterflies during the height of the summer. Lady's mantle, ribwort, anise, sorrel, violets, and many different types of clover are good sources of food for butterfly larvae.

Of course, leave as many weeds as possible undisturbed. Make sure they go into bloom, as long as they don't interfere with the vegetables and herbs in your garden.

Herbs That Attract Insects

Beekeepers, passionate nature lovers, and garden enthusiasts want to have gardens that attract beneficial insects. We all know how important the butterfly population and the bumblebee population are. And what better way to help them than to offer them a place that they can call home, where they can find food.

Borage attracts many insects.

Herbs in pots for the balcony and terrace.   *Herbs in a box on the balcony.*

Growing Herbs on Balconies and Terraces

Even if you don't have space for a garden, you can still grow herbs. Of course, the most important thing is full sun, whether you want to grow herbs for tea or to use as seasoning.

Places naturally protected by a fence or wall work particularly well. But even a roof can be a wonderful place to create an herb garden, as long as you can provide some protection from the wind and as long as there is sufficient water available. Rooftops are very windy at times, and temperatures can be very high.

Here are a few important tips to consider before starting a garden on your balcony:

• If there are no restrictions (perhaps in your lease), determine the weight that the balcony can accommodate before buying pots.
• If the balcony faces a street, do not hang flower pots or boxes on the outside of the railing.

• If the balcony does not have a gutter, use saucers or a tin lining to catch the overflow when you water your plants.
• Balconies that receive full sun are the best for growing herbs. If the balcony faces south, your plants will be grateful for some protection from the sun (such as shades) during the height of the summer season. The climate during spring and fall is the most comfortable on balconies that face east or west, and herbs grow very successfully there.
• High winds often damage plants on balconies, especially on upper floors. Ivy, growing on well-secured trellises, will protect plants without interfering with the aesthetic beauty of the garden. If size permits, larger bushes or miniature trees growing in containers, such as bay, rosemary, and other evergreens, also provide good protection from the wind.
• Just as an interior designer will make a sketch of the space to be furnished, you, too, should draw a plan for your balcony garden.
• Growing plants in plastic-lined burlap sacks is a very simple way of creating a garden on a balcony or a terrace.

An herb garden in a bag lined with foil or plastic.

Rosemary growing in an attractive container.

Ready-mixed potting soil left in the original bag works best. When using these sacks, make sure that you cut a few holes on the bottom for drainage. Place the bag on the floor and make round or cross cuts 8–10 inches (20–25 cm) apart on the top. These are the places where you'll plant the seedlings. Plants do exceedingly well in these "soil sacks." The only disadvantage is that they are only good for one year.

Containers

Many different containers are available for the movable herb garden. Some are even made from cement or plastic. In general, all these materials are okay. However, containers made from natural substances, such as stone, wood, ceramic, and pottery usually look better. When choosing containers, make sure that they complement the house in material, shape, and color, and that they blend well with the environment. Usually a plain container will work best; after all, it's the plant that you want to attract the attention.

Containers used outside must have sufficient drainage holes. If they are to remain outside during the winter, they should be able to withstand frost.

If you don't plan to move your movable herb garden, you may want to give it a permanent place on the terrace and remove the tile underneath it. Sitting directly on the ground allows the container to drain properly.

Soil

Potting soil is available in nurseries, but you can also mix your own. Use fifty percent garden soil, thirty to forty percent compost or bark humus, and ten to twenty percent sand. If the compost portion is to be fifty percent, make sure that the salt content does not exceed 0.1 oz per qt (3g per l). Test the soil after you mix it, so that you know the mixture is safe to use. Don't forget to add a layer of gravel or stones on the bottom for drainage.

Planting and Care

If a sufficiently large container is available, you can plant any combination of herbs as long as you consider the mature height of the plants. You can grow annuals as well as perennials in containers. However, remember that a container provides only a limited amount of space for the root system to grow, which also means a limited amount of water retention and nutrients.

For this reason, fertilize plants growing in a container at least every two to three weeks. Do this from the top. We prefer liquid compost teas (see page 29), diluted manure tea (see page 30), and commercial organic fertilizers, such as bone and blood meal.

Watering depends on the weather. In addition, you must adjust the watering schedule to the needs of the plants. This makes caring for movable herb gardens somewhat complicated.

Even more advantageous than the windowsill is a built-in window well made waterproof with a layer of plastic film. Here, seeds can grow directly into the soil in pots, bowls, or in saucers placed on top of the soil. Keep the soil moist in order to regulate the humidity in the window. Chives, chive garlic, and parsley are the plants that do best in such an environment.

Herb garden in front . . .

Growing Herbs in a Window

For year-round use, herbs do best in bright, east or west windows and in southern windows during the winter months. Gardeners can extend the available space in a window by covering radiators.

. . . and behind the window.

Growing chives:
1. Dig out healthy root balls and allow them to freeze.

2. Plant the root balls in a pot and place them in a window.

Growing Chives

The easiest way to grow chives is to take healthy plants from the garden. Allow the leaves to wilt and the root ball to freeze well. If the temperature in late fall does not bring sufficient frost, allow the root ball to dry out completely. You can stimulate the root ball in water at a temperature of 95–104°F (35–40°C) for about ten hours. Then plant the root ball and place it in the window garden. The tubelike leaves of this herb are more dependent on warmth than on light. After three cuts, the plant is usually exhausted but not spoiled. Replant it outside.

Growing Garlic

You only bring garlic plants inside for their spicy greens. Put several cloves in prepared soil in pots. Given sufficient water and kept at room temperature, leaves will grow rather quickly. You can harvest them repeatedly.

Garlic greens give many dishes (especially salads, yogurt, and cottage cheese) a gentle, refined, "French" flavor, considered the secret of many famous chefs.

Growing Parsley and Other Herbs

Planting parsley roots indoors isn't very complicated. Depending on the size, you can plant several roots in a deep pot. With moderate watering and moderate temperatures, parsley sprouts easily and grows well. When harvesting, remove only the outer leaves, assuring the plant a long life.

Of course, you can also pot parsley in late fall if you have a healthy plant with leaves. Place the pot in a window for winter use. However, sometimes this is not quite as successful as the root-ball method.

Sow dill and chervil in containers or bowls and place them in a window for use during the winter months. These

Harvested chives from a pot growing in the window.

herbs need sufficient daylight. Don't overwater them because they don't like "wet feet."

To make sure that enough green herbs are available throughout the winter months, many gardeners include white mustard, grown from seed, in their window herb gardens. Mustard germinates in pots or bowls in only a few days. You can harvest it three weeks later.

Cress is one of the herbs you can grow on "the fast track." Use flat, waterproof bowls or boxes filled with a thin layer of soil or line them with several layers of blotter or paper towels (not the perfumed type).

Be generous when seeding cress, and always keep the plants moist. The seeds will germinate (showing the first small leaves) in a few days. You can make the first cuts within ten days, when the leaves are about 2–2¼ inches (5–6cm) tall. The period from sewing to harvesting is short because the seeds contain all the nutrients necessary for healthy growth. Sow seeds every two weeks, and you will always have green cress available in the kitchen.

Growing cress is particularly educational for children. They especially enjoy watching a plant grow in an animal-shaped dish.

A cress animal.

A fragrant wreath used as a decoration.

Growing Herbs Inside

Herbs potted in pretty containers are beautiful focal points inside the house. Perennial teas and herbs used for seasoning (for instance upright and hanging fragrant geranium, bay, rosemary, thyme, lavender, sage, balm, oregano, and tarragon) are particular favorites for growing inside.

You can grow annual and biennial herbs in an indoor garden (see page 55).

Harvesting

Harvest herbs when the active substances within them are at their peak. When you want to use the leaves and flowers for medicinal purposes, the best time is just before the flowers open. This is the time when the chlorophyll and nutrients are at their peak. In some rare instances, harvesting takes place when the plant is in full bloom. You'll find specific information in "Plant Profiles" (starting on page 79).

Harvest fruit at their peak and seeds in the fall. Harvest roots, root balls, and bulbs after the leaves have died off, usually in late fall or, if you protect them during the winter, in the spring.

The best time to harvest herbs and flowers is before noon. If the plants are outside, wait until after the morning dew has evaporated. Collect seeds early in the morning, because fewer seeds are lost when the seed pods are ripe and fresh.

Make sure that you leave enough healthy leaves on the plant to allow new growth to take place. Always discard

The herb harvest is in full swing.

Harvest most herbs before the plants go into bloom.

Tie the herbs into bundles and hang them upside down to dry.

yellow, decaying leaves. Experienced herb gardeners allow freshly cut herbs to wilt in the sun immediately after cutting them. The drying process begins afterwards. This helps prevent spoilage.

Carefully scrub roots used for medicinal purposes, cut them into ⅜–¾ inch (1–2cm) pieces and dry them. You can store whole roots (unwashed) in sand or soil. Bundle or braid bulbs and hang them upside down or place them on racks in an airy place.

Wash fresh herbs quickly, but gently, under running water and shake them vigorously to remove as much excess water as possible.

Preserving

During the summer months, when the supply is abundant, carefully preserve herbs for use during the winter. Use the following old-fashioned methods.

Drying

This is the oldest and most widely used method of preserving herbs. Removing the water content inside the plant reduces sixty to ninety percent of its weight. Except for seed herbs, never dry herbs in the sun. Rather, tie them together in small bundles and hang them upside down in the airy part of a shed or lay them out on racks. If the leaves and flowers are very small, cover the racks with gauze or burlap. You need 11 square feet (1 sq m) of drying space for every 110 sq ft (10 sq m) of growing space.

Special dryers, in which a thermostat regulates the temperature, produce dried herbs of the highest quality.

Never expose herbs to direct sun when drying. Hang them in an airy room.

You can also dry herbs in boxes.

Sometimes it is necessary to dry herbs again during the off season. Use a dryer controlled by a thermostat.

Never expose herbs that contain essential oils to temperatures above 95–104°F (35–40°C) or the oils may evaporate.

The drying process is complete when the leaves make a rustling sound or when stems break off easily. This is the time when you crush the dried herbs (a sieve works well) and store them in airtight, clearly labelled containers. If you are planning to give the herbs as gifts, add information on how to use them to the labels.

The effectiveness of all herbs diminishes over time, regardless of how carefully you prepare and store them. Thus, we recommend that after one year, you discard the leaves and flowers of all

Freezing herbs:
1. Place finely chopped herbs in an ice-cube tray.

herbs dried for medicinal use. Replace them with freshly harvested and dried plants.

Freezing

You can also freeze many herbs. Parsley, dill, tarragon, chives, balm, and thyme work particularly well (see "Plant Profiles" starting on page 79).

Remove the rinsing water from freshly harvested herbs that you want to freeze. Make sure that you put them in the freezer immediately afterwards because otherwise they become soft and watery and loose many of their seasoning properties.

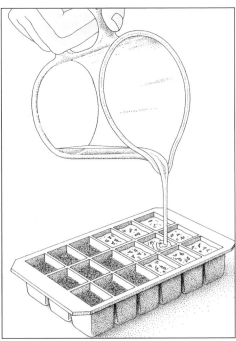

2. Add water and place the tray in the freezer.

3. Put the frozen cubes in small containers or freezer bags, label them, and store them in the freezer.

Here are several freezing methods:

• Place chopped herbs in ice-cube trays. Store the frozen cubes in containers or freezer bags.
• Wrap portions of herbs in foil, freeze; crumble before thawing them out.
• Freeze herbs whole in foil, remove from freezer, crush and crumble them quickly. Place them in a precooled container and immediately return them to the freezer.

Finely chop herbs and place them in a glass jar, alternating herbs and salt.

in wine vinegar or olive oil. Place the prepared herbs in a glass jar or container, add either wine vinegar or olive oil, and alternate herbs and liquid the same way you did with the salting method. Close, label, and store the container in a cool place.

Herbs suitable for preserving in vinegar include: basil, dill, tarragon, bay leaves, plants from the mint family, sage, chives, thyme, lemon balm, and onions.

Salting

For this, less popular, method, finely chop the herbs and place them in a glass or glazed-pottery container. Alternate a layer of salt with a layer of herbs. With this method, you can preserve a combination of herbs together. Use about 7 ounces (200g) of salt for each pound (kilogram) of herbs.

Seasoning in Vinegar and Oil

Finely chop freshly harvested and carefully rinsed herbs. Then immerse them

Preserve medicinal herbs in oil, vinegar, or wine.

To preserve herbs in oil, finely chop them and place them in a glass jar. Cover them with ¾in (2cm) of oil. Close the container and store it in a cool place.

Herbs in the Kitchen

The most important seasoning herbs are basil, dill, herbs from the mint family, garlic, bay, tarragon, anise, sage, chives, thyme, lemon balm, and onions.

Herb Jellies

Marmalades, jams, and jellies have a special flavor when you add fresh herbs, such as rosemary, sage, and thyme. Add these herbs before the fruit begins to boil. In the case of jellies, pour the hot mixture through a sieve and then allow it to set.

You can use other herbs, such as peppermint, parsley, and basil. The usual procedure is to brew a tea first and add it to the mixture instead of water. Herbal jellies usually use apples as the basic ingredient with the herbs adding their distinct flavor.

You can grow herbs for seasoning in pots.

Use tarragon jelly with fish and chicken, ruby-red rosemary jelly with turkey, and green basil jelly with beef. Add thyme to grape or elderberry jelly. Add marjoram and rosemary to citrus fruit jellies (orange, lemon, and grapefruit) and mint to gooseberry.

Herbal Butter

To make herbal butter, start by rubbing a generous amount of garlic in a bowl. Bring unsalted butter to room temperature. Mix these with finely chopped herbs, such as basil, dill, tarragon, chervil, a small amount of lovage, anise, lemon balm, and chives. Add a small amount of lemon juice and mix thoroughly.

Herbal Dips

You can use many different herbs to make an herbal dip. Take 18oz

Fresh herbs from the garden.

Basil is a favorite herb for herbal dips.

joram, 1 tablespoon (15ml) of pepper-corns, and a pinch of salt to 1 quart (1l) of olive oil. Keep the oil in a warm location for ten days, filter the contents, and pour them into a decorative bottle.

Homemade Herb Mixture for Pizza, Risotto, and Spaghetti

Mix equal parts of oregano, thyme, rosemary, sage, and basil and grind them in a mortar. When finished, add black pepper.

(500g) of whipped cottage cheese or yogurt and add ½ cup (113g) of sweet cream and ½ cup (113g) of hot water and mix to a creamy consistency. Next, add finely chopped herbs, such as dill, basil, garlic greens, garden cress, and purslane. Finally, add fresh tomatoes (cut in small cubes) and season with paprika and herbal vinegar.

Herbal Milk

Add prepared herbs—usually 4–5 tablespoons (60–75ml) of borage, dill, tarragon, chervil, parsley, a few celery leaves, and Jenny stonecrop—to 1 quart (1l) milk. Mix in a blender and pour into glasses.

Herbs à la Provence

Add a clove of crunched garlic, 1 tablespoon (15 ml) each of rosemary, thyme, savory, and mar-

Used with	Herbs
Roasts	basil, lovage, marjoram, mugwort, paprika, parsley, sage, savory, tarragon, thyme
Fowl	basil, dill, lovage, marjoram, mugwort, rosemary, savory, thyme
Fish	basil, celery, dill, horseradish, lovage, mustard (ground seeds), onions, parsley, rosemary, sage, savory
Game	basil, coriander, lovage, marjoram, rosemary, savory, thyme
Vegetables	anise, balm, basil, borage, chervil, chives, coriander, Jenny stonecrop, lovage, marjoram, onions, parsley, sage, savory, sorrel, tarragon
Raw vegetables	anise, balm, basil, borage, chives, dill, garlic, horseradish, lovage, onions, parsley, sorrel, tarragon
Salads	anise, balm, basil, borage, chives dill, fennel, Jenny stonecrop, onions, parsley, rocket, savory, sorrel, tarragon, thyme
Sauces and gravies	balm, basil, chervil, dill, leek, lovage, marjoram, oregano, peppermint, savory
Soups	basil, celery, chervil, dill, leeks, lovage, paprika, parsley, purslane, savory, sorrel

Mixed Herbs

You can combine different dried herbs for a homemade herb mixture. Fine herbs include: basil, savory, chervil, marjoram, oregano, rosemary, and sage. Bouquets garnis include three or more herbs, such as parsley, thyme, and bay, tied together in small bouquets.

The seven herbs used in a green sauce: chervil, anise, chives, parsley, borage, cress, and sorrel.

Herbal Alternatives to Salt and Pepper

To make your own homemade seasoning salt, finely grind tarragon, parsley, leek, sage, and onions and mix with sea salt. Keep this herbal salt uncovered in a cool place.

Make an alternative to black pepper by mixing equal parts of basil, savory, and a small amount of rosemary, according to taste.

Herbal Bread

When baking flat bread or herbal rolls,

A green sauce.

add one or a combination of the following to the dough: fennel, coriander, caraway seeds, flaxseeds, poppy seeds, rosemary, thyme. Cookies taste great when you add anise seeds and sweet woodruff.

Herbs for a Green Sauce

You can make a special German sauce, called a green sauce, with seven fresh herbs: borage, chervil, garden cress, parsley, anise, sorrel, and chives.

You'll need about 7 ounces (200g) of this mixture to serve four people. Rinse the herbs, pat them dry, and finely chop them. Combine the herbs with sour cream or milk and mix to a creamy consistency in a blender. If you like, you can add the juice of one lemon, a small amount of fruit vinegar, 4½oz (125g) mayonnaise, or 2 small cups of yogurt. Also add a little salt, pepper, sugar, and mustard, depending on your taste.

This will cover eight hard-boiled eggs, cut in half and arranged on a platter. Decorate the plate with fresh herbs. Serve with boiled potatoes, cold meat, or on toast.

Preparing Herbs for the Kitchen and the Medicine Cabinet

Recipes for Medicinal Herbs

1. Seasoned Wine: Use a handful of different herbs for each quart (liter) of wine. Mix in a glazed pottery crock (left), keep in a dark place for several days, and then separate the wine from the herbs (right).

2. Fresh Juices: To make a fresh herb juice, chop fresh herbs, for instance, stinging nettle (far left), and squeeze out the juices (right). You can also pour these juices into ice-cube trays (left) and freeze for later use.

3. Tinctures: Cover selected herbs with one bottle of spirits or wine (above left) and leave to cure, shaking the bottle frequently (above right). After about two weeks, separate the wine from the herbs (below left), fill a bottle, and store.

4. Medicinal Salve: (from top to bottom) Heat fresh or dried herbs in oil (almond oil, for instance) and pour through a sieve. To make a salve, melt beeswax in a pot and mix it with the herbal oil.

Recipes for the Kitchen

5. Fine Herbs: A traditional French mixture, grind together: basil, savory, chervil, marjoram, parsley, rosemary, and chives.

6. Frozen Herbs: Mix finely chopped herbs with a little water in an ice-cube tray, and freeze.

7. Herbs in Salt: Layer finely chopped herbs with salt in a glass container, 7oz (200g) of salt for every pound (1kg) of herbs. Close and store in a cool place.

8. Herbs in Flavored Oils: Cover finely chopped herbs with olive oil, add enough for the oil to extend about ¾in (2cm) above the herbs.

Herbs for Medicinal Purposes

Since ancient times, people have extracted healing substances and essential oils from plants and used them for medicinal purposes.

Decorative, healing herbs: great mullein, chamomile, marigold, hollyhocks, lady's mantle, cotton lavender, lavender, Jenny stonecrop, meadowsweet, and hyssop.

Herbal Oils

You can make most of the popular herbal oils at home, using, for instance, peppermint, rose of Sharon, lavender, dill, thyme, rosemary, and lemon balm. The essential oils are soluble in fatty oils, such as olive, sunflower, or almond oil. You can easily extract them.

Add a handful of herbs to a quart (liter) of good oil (preferably olive oil) and cure for two to three weeks in full sun, shaking the container frequently. The substances you want to extract will permeate the olive oil. St.-John's-Wort changes the color to a dark red.

Effects of the Most Important Medicinal Garden Herbs

Indication	Medicinal Herbs
Respiratory (colds)	anise, black elderberry, coltsfoot, garden sage, hollyhocks, hyssop, marjoram, oregano, primrose, ribwort, tall anise, thyme
Stomach and intestine	basil, caraway seeds, elecampane, garlic, German chamomile, lovage, medicinal fennel, peppermint, yarrow
Appetite and digestion	anise, bee balm, centaury, chervil, coriander, cress, dill, mugwort, parsley, rosemary, sage, sorrel, tarragon, verbena
Laxative	castor oil and flaxseed oil
Relaxation and sleeping	black elderberry, dragonhead, German chamomile, lavender, lemon balm, lime flower, St.-John's-Wort, sweet woodruff, valerian
Heart and circulation	balm, garlic, lavender, motherwort, rosemary, valerian
Liver and gallbladder	dandelion, plants from the mint family, rosemary, yarrow
Kidney and bladder	borage, garden chervil, oregano, parsley, stinging nettle, tall anise, tarragon
Muscles	marigold, parsley, tall nettle, yarrow
Treatment of external wounds	aloe vera, comfrey, German chamomile, marigold, yarrow
Headaches	black elderberry, lemon balm, peppermint

A basket of herbs for seasoning and medicinal uses.

Hollyhocks, with an attractive flower.

After the oils have cured properly, pour them through a fine-mesh sieve. Squeeze out the excess oil and fill the rest into attractive bottles. You can increase the effectiveness and concentration of the oils by adding fresh herbs to oil you have already cured once and allowing it to go through the same process again.

Herbal oils, such as arnica, lavender, rosemary, great mullein flower, balm, and mint oils, are particularly effective for external use as massage oils. You can also use them as bath oils and for natural skin care. Use oils made from marigold, St.-John's-Wort, marshmallow, fenugreek, and rosemary.

You can make healing mouthwashes from sage, mint, balm, and sunflower oil. They are effective in cases of gum inflammation, loose teeth, and bad breath.

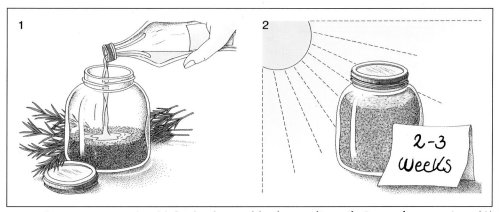

To make a massage oil, add finely chopped herbs to olive oil. Cover the container (1) and cure in full sun (2), stirring frequently. After two to three weeks, pour the oil through a sieve to remove the herbs.

Herbal Spirits

Herbal spirits, herbal liquor, and homemade medicines have always been very popular and effective homemade remedies. After a heavy meal, in case of an upset stomach, as well as in countless other situations, herbal spirits have proven to be quite reliable.

Making the spirits is really very simple. Those with experience recommend the use of liquor or brandy bottles with a wide opening. Place the herbs in the bottle (a good handful will do) and add brandy or clear spirits that are at least thirty percent proof. Replace the cork and place the bottle in full sun, shaking it frequently. After two to three weeks, pour the liquid through a sieve and then back into the bottle.

St.-John's-Wort for herbal spirits.

Spirits have a long shelf life. If you like sweetened spirits, dissolve sugar in boiling water or add maple syrup to the mixture.

Medicinal and Seasoning Wines

To make herbal wines, add 1–1½oz (30–40g) of herbs to every quart (liter) of white, red, or sweet wine. Glass containers or glazed pottery jugs work best. Place the closed container in a dark location at room temperature.

After several days, your homemade medicinal or seasoning wine separates from the herbs and is ready for drinking.

When properly prepared, the shelf life of these wines ranges from several months for red and white wines to several years for sweet wines.

The following herb combinations work well for herbal spirits: lemon balm, lovage, plants from the mint family, arnica, rosemary, hyssop, mugwort (in small amounts), and thyme. Herbs used for homemade herbal and medicinal wines: sweet woodruff (in small amounts), basil, rosemary, lemon balm, mugwort (in small amounts), hyssop (in small amounts), herbs from the mint family, lavender, chamomile, and other herbs.

Fresh Juices from Herbs

The best known of the fresh-squeezed juices is stinging-nettle juice. Among

Shepherd's purse.

the herbs used to make spring cleansing juices are watercress, verbena, anise, and other weed herbs, such as shepherd's purse, dandelion, and hops. Try to use the herbs as quickly as possible after you harvest them. Of course, you'll need to carefully rinse them and pat them dry. If time is a problem, you may temporarily freeze them. Always dilute fresh herbal juices with water, mineral water, or yogurt. Use freshly pressed juices immediately.

Tinctures and Plant Extracts in Alcohol

To make a tincture, use fresh, dried, or pulverized herbs. Place the herbs in a bottle, add spirits, close the bottle, and allow the mixture to cure for about fourteen days, shaking the contents frequently. Pour the mixture through a strainer and place the tincture in carefully labelled bottles. You can add these tinctures, a few drops at a time, to hot or cold drinks, such as tea. Most of the time, however, you'll want to dilute them in water and use them externally for compresses or add them to a footbath.

Herbal Salves and Creams

Herbal salves, made with oils or similar substances, are very soothing. You can make them from fresh or dried herbs. You can also use herbal tinctures or oils (for recipes see page 74). Gently heat the raw material with fatty substances, such as lanolin, almond oil, or lard. Add beeswax to give the mixture a solid consistency.

You can extend the shelf life of the preparations by sealing the surface with a layer of paraffin. Store these homemade preparations in the refrigerator. But even with this method of storage, discard unused portions after a few weeks.

Homemade Poultices

You can puree many herbs, such as ribwort, marjoram, and garlic (also onions, carrots, potatoes, and even cabbage leaves), spread them on a clean cloth, and use them as poultices to treat bruises, contusions, sprains, and similar injuries. Do not apply poultices to open wounds.

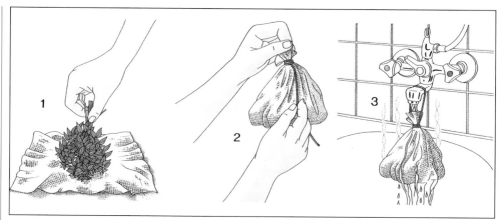

Preparing herbs for a relaxing bath: (1) Place herb cutting in gauze wrapping. (2) Tie the wrapping to form a bag. (3) Suspend the bag from the faucet and run hot water through it.

Herbs for the Bath

Adding medicinal herbs from your own garden to a tub filled with warm water is one of the most comfortable ways to relax. You can use a single herb or a combination of them for a very specific effect. Wrap 3½ ounces (100g) of the herbs in a piece of gauze or muslin and tie it under the faucet as the water fills the tub.

Herbs for the bath:

Valerian for sleeplessness and tension

Chamomile for skin disorders and hemorrhoids

Lavender to relieve tension in cases of low blood pressure

Balm for nervousness and nervous heart problems

Rosemary for low blood pressure

Thyme for respiratory problems

Other favorite herbs are yarrow, herbs from the mint family, and gold balm.

Lavender prepared for the bath induces a calming effect.

The Most Important Herbs for the Home Pharmacy

Common Name (Botanical Name)	Indications	Usage	Daily Dose
Elderberry (*Sambucus nigra*)	Colds, flu, increased perspiration	Tea from flowers: 1 tsp. (5ml) per cup Tea from berries: 1 tsp. (5ml) per cup	3–5 cups 3 cups
St.-John's-Wort (*Hypericum perforatum*)	Nervousness, insomnia, to strengthen nerves	Tea: 2 tsp. (10ml) per cup	2 cups
German chamomile (*Chamomilla recutita*)	Stomach and intestinal flu, flatulence, colds, bronchitis, infections	Tea: 2 tsp. (10ml) per cup	3 cups As an inhalant, inhale often for four–six weeks
Mint family (*Mentha* fam.)	Stomach and intestinal flu, poor digestion, flatulence, to strengthen gallbladder	Tea: 2 tsp. (10ml) per cup	2–3 cups for two–three weeks only
	Oils: neuralgia, rheumatism, headache	Rub on skin	As indicated
Rosemary (*Rosmarinus officinalis*)	Stomach, intestines, gallbladder (*not during pregnancy*)	Tea: 1 tsp. (5ml) per cup	Sip 1 cup morning and night
	For bath: circulatory problems, rheumatism	Boil 1¾oz (50g) in 1 quart (liter) water	
Sage (*Salvia officinalis*)	Stomach and intestinal pain, nausea, diarrhea, loss of appetite	Tea: 2 tsp. (10ml) per cup	2–3 cups
Ribwort (*Plantago lanceolata*)	Cough, hoarseness Insect bites, bruises	Tea: 1–2 tsp. (5–10ml) per cup Poultice of chopped leaves	3 cups several times daily
Centaury (*Centaurium erythraea*)	Weak stomach, digestive and gallbladder problems, loss of appetite	Tea: 1 tsp. (5ml) per cup	Sip 2 cups throughout the day
Thyme (*Thymus vulgaris*)	Bronchitis, stomach and intestinal problems, colds	Tea: 1 tsp. (5ml) per cup	Sip 2 cups throughout the day
Vermouth (*Artemisia absinthium*)	Upset stomach, gallbladder problems, loss of appetite, flatulence (*not during pregnancy; toxic in larger amounts*)	Tea: ½ tsp. (2.5ml) per cup As wine: ½–¾oz (15–20g) in 24oz (0.7l)	Sip 2 cups throughout the day 1 shot glass
Lemon balm (*Melissa officinalis*)	Nervousness, insomnia, nervous stomach and intestines, headache	Tea: 2 tsp. (10ml) per cup	1 cup morning and evening

Herbal tea: (1) Rinse a cup with hot water. (2) Place the proper amount of herbs in a teapot, using a bag or sieve. Add boiling water, cover the pot, and let steep for ten to fifteen minutes. (3) Remove the bag or insert.

Using Herbal Teas

Medicinal teas should not contain more than four different herbs. One plant should be the major ingredient; the others increase its effectiveness. If it is necessary to improve the taste and appearance, you may add one or two more herbs.

Well-known herbal teas include: thyme for bronchitis, chicory and yarrow for the gallbladder, tea with vermouth for upset stomach, elderberry and lime blossom for colds, sage and German chamomile for a sore throat, and valerian and balm to calm nerves.

Herbs for everyday use include: German chamomile, herbs from the mint family, lemon balm, lime blossom, raspberry, blackberry, strawberry, leaves from the black raspberry bush, and flowers from the elderberry bush.

Poured over ice, herbal teas are wonderful thirst quenchers on a hot summer day. The following are very popular: herbs from the mint family, lemon balm, blackberry leaves, fennel, flowers from the elderberry bush, as well as any combination of these. The most popular additions to summertime tea are lemon, other fruit juices, and even mineral water.

To improve taste and color, you may add the following: leaves from black raspberry, flowers from the elderberry, apple peel, hollyhock, and yarrow.

Sweeten these teas with sugar, honey, or an artificial sweetener while hot or served cold over ice. Mix them, if desired, with different fruit juices or with a slice of pineapple or orange.

Making Natural Cosmetics from Herbs

Nature provides us with a whole array of substances that add to our well-being, grace, and beauty. Natural cosmetics are made from all or part of a fresh plant. They include the following: pureed berries, pureed parsley green, or carrots for facial masks; watercress and chlorophyll masks combined with different herbs for facial lotions. In general, natural cosmetics contain plant material prepared prior to being added to a base.

Follow these basic rules in order to avoid problems and disappointments later:

• Use only plants grown organically and never those that grow close to high-traffic areas or industrial complexes.
• As a base, use only high-quality products sold in a drugstore or a pharmacy.
• Do not expect instant results when using natural products. Effects that are noticeable only after repeated, constant use usually last longer.
• Since natural, homemade creams salves, and balms don't contain preservatives, they have only a limited shelf life, even when stored in the refrigerator. Therefore, make only enough for what you need and always use it when fresh. Neither your home-grown ingredients nor the carefully prepared product you make in your home can prevent the development of bacteria and fungi—sometimes in only a few days.
• The most appropriate containers are those made out of glass, ceramics, or glazed pottery. All metals, even those that have a coat, attack the ingredients in your products.

Basic Recipes for Homemade Cosmetics

Marigold Cream:
Allow 7 ounces (200g) of lard to melt over low heat, add a handful of marigold flowers, stir well, and then set aside to cool. After twenty-four hours, melt again over low heat, pour through a sieve, and fill a glass jar with a wide neck.

Elderberry-flower Cream for Smooth, Soft Skin:
Mix ¼ cup (50ml) of almond oil (or any other suitable oil) with 4 teaspoons (20ml) of lanolin, 1 teaspoon (5ml) of honey, and 2 tablespoons (30ml) of dried elderberry flower. Warm this mixture for thirty minutes over a low flame and pour into a jar.

Elderberry flowers are dried for use in the cream recipe.

Herbal Lotion:

Soak a handful of fresh chamomile, elderberry, or linden flowers in ⅓ cup (75 ml) milk, buttermilk, or whey for about three hours. Pour the lotion through a sieve and let it drain well. Place over low heat and let the lotion warm up gently. Add 1 teaspoon (5ml) of honey, allow to cool, fill a bottle, and store in a refrigerator. Lotion will keep for one week.

Arnica Tincture:

Pour 16oz (0.5l) of forty-percent alcohol in a bottle, add a good handful of arnica flowers, and close the bottle tightly. Allow the contents to cure at room temperature for fourteen days, shaking the bottle frequently. Pour through a sieve, squeeze the flowers thoroughly, and replace in the bottle.

Herbal Masks:

Pour 8oz (0.25l) of boiling-hot milk over a handful of whole herbs, such as thyme, anise, parsley, rosemary, or watercress. Spread the herbs out on a milk-soaked bandage and place on the skin for fifteen minutes. Use on the neck, throat, etc.

Decorating with Herbs

The following are examples of how you can use fragrant herbs in a multitude of ways. Of course, you can develop your own ideas.

When the supply of fragrant plants and flowers is at its height in the spring and summer, you have a wonderful opportunity to make decorative items for use as gifts or for your own home.

Fragrant Pillows and Pouches

For fragrant pillows and pouches, crush herbs with particularly delicate or popular fragrances and use them to

Fragrant pouches: (1) Dry herbs first. (2) Use them to fill a small pouch. (3) Place them in decorative pillows for gifts.

fill pouches made from linen, silk, or other cloth that allows the aroma to escape. By creating clever shapes, perhaps a "sleeping roll," you can make very attractive and very personal gifts in no time at all. You may want to make an additional cover so that you can easily change it when the original cover needs laundering. You can take aromatic pillows on a trip, and you can wear very small ones on your body.

Dried herbs for a potpourri: lavender, oregano, sage, chamomile, rosemary, and others.

Sleeping Pillows

Aromatic sleeping pillows usually contain lavender, lemon balm, fennel, dill, lemon thyme, different herbs from the mint family, strawflowers, hops, and a little valerian.

When you expose the herbs, they release their essential oils, according to the body's temperature, often providing very restful sleep.

Herbs for Fragrant Pouches

Fill rose pouches with rose leaves and add a small amount of mint and clove powder. Fill lemon pouches with lemon balm, lemon thyme, lemon verbena, and just a hint of valerian. Fern pouches are very beneficial for lumbago and sciatica. Strawflower pouches relieve intestinal cramps.

Moth-repellent Pouches

Fill fragrant pouches, also called moth sacks, with wormwood, sweet woodruff, mint, rosemary, lavender, and thyme. They will repel moths in closets.

Potpourris

Potpourri is a collection of colorful, fragrant, dried herbs in a decorative glass. Depending on the aroma and color effect you desire, you can create personal aroma accents with the following fragrant flowers: roses, carnations, heliotrope, chamomile, elderberry, lavender, marigold, cornflower, bee balm, jasmine, and wallflower.

The most popular aromatic leaves are those from the mint family, balm, sweet woodruff, rosemary, sage, thyme, tarragon, basil, lemon balm, and garden reseda.

To increase a particular fragrance, you might want to add 1–2 tablespoons (15–30ml) of ground-up anise seeds, whole cloves, chestnut, coriander, ground nutmeg, cinnamon sticks, or lemon or orange peel to every quart (liter) of mixture.

Potpourri in a closed glass container is very decorative, and when you remove the lid, it adds a wonderful summer fragrance to any indoor environment.

Potpourri: (1) Combine fragrant leaves and flowers according to your taste. Fragrant seeds or the like intensify the fragrance. (2) Place all in a glass container. Lifting the cover releases wonderful aromas.

Colorful potpourris:

   Green: leaves from wormwood, bay, balm, herbs from the mint family, rosemary, sage, sweet woodruff, lemon balm, lemon thyme.

   White: jasmine flowers, carnation, snow bells, roses, white clover.

   Blue: flowers from borage, dragon's head, violet, heliotrope, catnip, lavender, rosemary, hyssop.

   Red and pink: flowers from oregano, germander, hollyhock, carnation, roses.

   Yellow: flowers from German chamomile, garden reseda, roses.

Fragrant Tumbler

You can create a fragrant tumbler by placing fresh aromatic herbs in a container that you can close tightly. Favorite herbs include fresh leaves from wormwood, flowers from roses and reseda, as well as sage, hyssop, the flowers from lavender and wallflower, thyme, ground lemon peel, cloves, and iris roots. Add pure alcohol as a fixative. After mixing all ingredients, place the tumbler in a dark location for a couple of weeks while the plants and flowers release their refreshing aromas.

Fragrant Balls

Make fragrant balls, perfect for hanging in different places in the house, from fine-mesh wire, filled with peat moss and aromatic herbs, similar to those used for a potpourri (see page 77) and a fragrant tumbler.

Plant Profiles

Herb Descriptions Listed Alphabetically by Botanical (Latin) Name

In general, we use the herbs we grow in our gardens for very mild medicinal benefits, for seasoning food, or for their pleasant fragrances.

What follows is a description of a number of herbs, listed alphabetically by their botanical names, indicating if they are perennials or annuals and the height of the mature plant. The family name follows the botanical name.

The list also includes information about the medicinal benefits of the herbs. The recommended dose pertains only to the particular herb being discussed.

Only take natural medicines for a limited time. Never take them longer than necessary. Change homemade teas often. Only treat minor health problems that do not need professional medical treatment. The suggestions in this book are not a substitute for a visit to your physician.

Yarrow
Achillea millefolium
Compositae

This is a medicinal plant with characteristics similar to German chamomile (see page 97).

Characteristics: Perennial; grows up to 27in (69cm) tall; blooms from June on; white, sometimes reddish white flowers; faint scent.

Active substances: Essential oils with bitters and flavonoid.

Cultivation: Sunny location; undemanding; sow seeds in spring in rows about 16in (40cm) apart; also propa-

gate by dividing older plants; red- and yellow-blooming varieties have less medicinal value. Companion planting: other herbaceous perennials.

Harvesting: Young leaves starting in May; flowers or flowering stems from June until October.

Culinary: Tender shoots and leaves in early spring in salad.

Medicinal: Relieves cramps and infections; improves appetite, relieves minor stomach problems, including cramp-like conditions; reduces intestinal and gallbladder problems.

People with known allergies to plants from the Compositae family might also be allergic to this plant and should not use it.

Cosmetics: Cleansing and soothing for oily skin with large pores; also used for hair.

Yarrow.

Onion
Allium cepa et al.
Liliaceae

People have grown onions since ancient times.

Characteristics: Annual, seasonal plant, often continues through several seasons; grows up to 8–32in (20–80cm) tall; leaves called shallots; outer, dry skin of the onion can be brownish, red, or white.

Active Substances: Sulfur-containing combinations similar to garlic but in different combinations and concentrations; minerals; and vitamin C.

Cultivation: Prefers full sun; light, humus-containing soil, not freshly fertilized; additional feeding usually not necessary.

Companion planting: carrots, salads, and kohlrabi.

Shallots—Allium ascalonicum: Propagate with bulbs, 4 × 8in (10 × 20cm) apart; also possible from seeds, 6 × 10in (15 × 25cm) apart.

   Onion—Allium cepa: Propagate from seeds, 8 × 10in (20 × 25cm) apart; from bulbs, 4 × 8in (10 × 20cm) apart.

   Top onion—Allium cepa var. *viviparum:* Propagate with small seeds or bulb onions; also possible by division.

   Welsh onion—Allium fistulosum: Propagate through division, also from seeds.

Harvesting: Regular onion in first year after growth has stopped and leaves have become dry. Tie several together and air dry. All above-mentioned varieties produce shallots.

Culinary: Multiple uses, fresh as well as dried, for almost every conceivable dish: soups, sauces, salads, etc.

Medicinal: Stimulates appetite and digestion, is a diuretic, used for colds and coughs.

Cosmetics: Dilute tincture (see page 71) controls hair loss and blemishes (*but use with care*).

Onions.

Top onions.

Garlic.

Garlic
Allium sativum
Liliaceae

Garlic is one of the herbs people grew in ancient times.

Characteristics: Compound bulbs, usually with several smaller cloves curving around one main clove; grows up to 12–28in (30–70cm) tall.

Rocambole, Italian garlic, gourmet garlic—*Allium sativum* var. *ophioscorodon:* smaller, more delicate version of regular garlic.

Active Substances: Sulfur-containing combinations that release a strong aroma when cut; vitamins B and C and minerals.

Cultivation: Sunny location; nutrient- and humus-rich soil, not freshly fertilized; propagate in spring with cloves 8in (20cm) apart set in rows 6in (15cm) apart; planting so-called seed bulbs that develop next to usually infertile flowers delays harvest for one year; will grow in containers.

Companion planting: cucumbers, potatoes, salads, carrots, beets, spinach, and tomatoes; avoid planting near bush and pole beans, peas, cabbages, and kohlrabi.

Harvesting: Remove from soil and place in sun after leaves turn yellow and fall over, tie or braid them together and hang upside down in a cool dry place.

Culinary: Fresh leaves as seasoning, as chives; add crushed cloves to many different dishes: sauces, soups, salads; also use with oil and vinegar for salad dressing.

Medicinal: Supports digestion; disinfects intestines; lowers blood pressure; prevents age-related diseases. Externally: crushed and mixed with mineral water, milk, yogurt, or kefir, use for skin disorders (*with caution*).

Chive
Allium schoenoprasum
Liliaceae

Characteristics: Perennial; grows up to 8–12in (20–30cm) tall; has onionlike scent.

Active Substances: Same as those in onions (see page 81).

Cultivation: Sunny to partial shade; high in nutrients; will tolerate damp and chalky soil; propagate with seeds in rows 10in (25cm) apart and by dividing; set divided plants 8 × 8in (20 × 20cm) apart; planting a root ball in a pot also works well (see page 54).

Chives.

Chive garlic.

Companion planting: carrots and all shrublike herbs. Don't plant close to other onionlike herbs.

Harvesting: Can be cut in garden beginning in April; preserve by freezing or drying.

Culinary: Usually fresh and added to salads, sauces, cottage cheese, meat dishes, eggs, potatoes; do not boil chives.

Medicinal: Stimulates appetite; supports digestion.

Cultivation: Sunny location; humus, sandylike soil; propagate in rows, 10in (25cm) apart; move plants indoors in fall; from January on, does well in pots, similar to chives (see page 56).

Harvesting: Only while fresh.

Culinary: Fresh herbs as seasoning for almost any food.

Medicinal: As for garlic and onions.

Ramsons (Bear's Garlic)
Allium ursinum
Liliaceae

The whole plant, particularly after blooming, has an intense garlic–leek scent.

Characteristics: Perennial; grows up to 20in (50cm) tall; white flowers from April to June; bulbs are almost white and up to 2½in (6cm) long with very few companion bulbs (photo, page 84).

Active Substances: Sulfur-containing combinations, as in garlic, but different in composition.

Chive Garlic
Allium tuberosum
Liliaceae

Characteristics: Biennial; grows up to 8–12in (20–30cm) tall; has onion–garlic aroma.

Active Substances: Sulfur-containing combinations as in onions (see page 81).

Ramsons (bear's garlic).

Cultivation: Partially shady locations; humus soil; propagate with seeds in spring.

Harvesting: Continuous; use freshly cut individual leaves until bloom, to protect plant; use harvested leaves in dried form or in teas, before blooming until May.

Culinary: Young leaves used as garlic; finely chopped in cottage cheese, for salads, sauces, soups, and vegetables; flavor is less than that of garlic.

Medicinal: Similar to garlic, but preferred for digestive problems and loss of appetite; careful external use for skin problems.

Aloe Vera
Aloe vera (Aloe barbardensis)
Liliaceae

Characteristics: Perennial; grows up to 24 inches (60cm) tall; succulent plant with fleshy, spiny leaves that contain a bitter, slimy, yellowish white juice.

The *A. saponaria* and others from the Aloe family have medicinal properties similar to those of the *Aloe vera*.

Active Substances: Aloin and mucilage.

Cultivation: Undemanding indoor plant; water sparingly; transfer outside to the herb garden in the summer; depending on size, plant 16–20in (40–50cm) apart in a sunny location; bring indoors before the first frost; very little watering during winter months; propagate through cuttings.

Harvesting: Always use lower leaves, which will stay fresh for several days in the refrigerator.

Medicinal: Relieves pain; inhibits infections; promotes wound healing. Use the mucus externally for insect bites, sunburn, and minor injuries of the skin; also effective against muscle cramps, sore joints, and arthritis.

Aloe (Aloe vera).

Aloe saponaria.

Lemon verbena.

Cosmetic: Component of numerous moisturizers in cosmetic preparations. Cut away outer skin of leaf, slice open and place (mucus side down) on affected area of the skin.

Lemon Verbena
Aloysia triphylla
Verbenaceae (Vervain family)

Characteristics: Shrub; grows up to 6½ft (2m) tall; not winter-hardy; shrublike growth; blooms from June to fall; leaves have a lemony scent.
Active Substances: Essential oils, flavonoid, and minerals.
Cultivation: Sunny locations as container plant; transfer outside to the herb garden (usually as an individual plant) during summer; propagate by cuttings taken during the summer months or by layering; water and fertilize moderately; protect from rust; prune back once a year.
Harvesting: Fresh leaves and young shoots as needed, but not during winter months; collect leaves for drying in late summer, keep in airtight containers.
Culinary: To flavor desserts, baked goods, and fruit juices; in dried form, used in fragrant pouches.
Medicinal: As tea, reduces minor digestive problems and acts as a sedative; improves taste of medicinal mixtures. *Use only in small amounts and not over a prolonged period of time.*
Cosmetic: Refreshing when added to the bath.

Marshmallow
Althaea officinalis
Malvaceae

Marshmallow is a beautiful wild plant with white or pink flowers that bloom from June to September in the northern hemisphere.
Characteristics: Perennial; grows up to 5ft (1.5m) tall; faint fragrance (see photo, page 86).
Active Substances: Mucilage and traces of essential oils in leaves.

Marshmallow.

Dill in bloom.

Cultivation: Sunny, warm locations; prefers damp and heavy soil; very undemanding; propagate through division and seeds in spring, allowing for ample room, at least 20 × 30in (50 × 80cm).

Harvesting: Flowers during the summer months; leaves from May to July; roots from October to April (in the northern hemisphere); store roots and dried leaves in glass containers or cans.

Dill seeds.

Medicinal: Promotes healing of respiratory system: cough, hoarseness; relieves stomach and intestinal problems.
Cosmetic: In a salve, soothes and smoothes irritated, chapped, and infected skin; also good for treating skin blemishes.

Dill
Anethum graveolens
Umbelliferae

The dill plant has a characteristic scent and flavor all its own. The seeds taste somewhat like caraway seeds.
Characteristics: Annual; grows up to 40in (1m) tall; yellow flowers from June to August in the northern hemisphere.
Active Substances: Essential oils, mucus substances, resins, and tannic acid.
Cultivation: Sunny locations; warm, humus soil; sow in rows 10in (25cm) apart starting in April and continuing throughout summer; for best results, choose a new location every year; will grow in a pot.

Because snails will avoid dill, these plants are important for companion planting with: bush and pole beans, cucumbers, asparagus, potatoes, cabbage, kohlrabi, lettuce, carrots, beets, celery, tomatoes, and onions.

Harvesting: Cut first leaves and shoots four to six weeks after sowing, continue throughout summer and fall until first frost.

Culinary: Fresh, dried, and frozen used for salads, vegetables, soups, sauces, raw fruit, vegetables, tomatoes, fish, meat, and pickles; seeds used as caraway seeds for seasoning.

Medicinal: Increases appetite; supports digestion; relieves cramps.

Angelica
Angelica archangelica
Umbelliferae

The plant has a strong, spicy fragrance, and the greenish white flowers have a honey scent.

Characteristics: Biennial; grows up to 6½ft (2m) tall; blooms in July and August in the northern hemisphere.

Active Substances: Essential oils and bitter substances.

Cultivation: Sunny or partially shady locations; deep enough in the soil, sufficiently moist; needs lots of room to grow in the second year, 20 × 24in (50 × 60cm); in late summer, sow seeds in rows at least 20in (50cm) apart; feed now and then with compost.

Harvesting: Fresh shoots from June on; fall of the second year, after plant dies back, take root ball; store dried in glass container.

Culinary: Fresh leaves and stems to flavor soups, sauces, salads; roots for teas, liquor, and herbal spirits.

Medicinal: As tea, relieves stomach and intestinal problems, such as flatulence, bloating, and minor cramplike complaints; improves appetite.

When using angelica, do not sunbath because the plant contains light-sensitive substances.

Angelica.

Angelica roots.

A nonblooming garden chervil.

Chervil in bloom.

Chervil
Anthriscus cerefolium
Umbelliferae

Chervil is an aromatic, sweet, aniselike spice.

Characteristics: Annual; grows up to 28in (70cm) tall; white flowers starting in May (in the northern hemisphere); faint scent.

Active Substances: Essential oils with glycoside and bitters.

Cultivation: Sunny to partially shady locations; loose soil, moderately moist; sow in rows at least 6 inches (15cm) apart, continue throughout the season, starting in March; also grows well in boxes and pots.

Companion planting: bush beans, endives, lettuces, and radishes.

Harvesting: Young shoots, leaves, and flowers May till December; use chervil fresh.

Culinary: Fresh green chervil (also frozen or dried) for soups, sauces, cottage cheese, egg dishes, potatoes, herbal butter, and cheeses; don't boil.

Medicinal: Increases appetite; supports blood cleansing and metabolism; is a diuretic.

Cosmetic: For facial lotion, make a decoction with the herb.

Horseradish
Armoracia rusticana
Cruciferae

Horseradish grows in temperate climates all over the world.

Characteristics: Perennial, but usually grown as an annual; grows up to 4ft (1.2m) wide; white flowers; strong central roots and smaller side roots; propagate abundantly; roots have a sharp, biting taste.

Active Substances: Sulphur compounds, vitamin C, and minerals.

Cultivation: Sunny to partially shady locations; provide deeply cultivated soil with enough moisture-retaining material; feed moderately with compost; propagate from single root stalks 6–8in (15–20cm) long, place thin side roots in a row 12–16in (30–40cm) apart begin-

Horseradish in bloom.

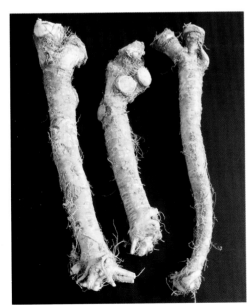

Horseradish roots.

ning in March, remove subsequent side roots frequently during summer months so that the main root can develop a beautiful single root stalk; needs mulch.

Companion planting: very useful with potatoes.

Harvesting: Dig roots up in fall; store in sand in cool basement.

Culinary: Roots (freshly ground or frozen) for mixing with sour cream or sweet cream, delicious with meat and fish dishes, tomato, cottage cheese; also used to make homemade mustard; roots added when pickling.

Medicinal: Supports digestion; is a diuretic; *for those with stomach problems, use carefully.* For external use in case of skin disorders; *use with great caution because of effects on the skin.*

Arnica
Arnica montana
Compositae

Characteristics: Perennial; grows up to 24in to (60cm) tall; orange-yellow flowers, brown root stock (see photo, page 90).

Active Substances: Flavonoid and essential oils.

Cultivation: Sunny locations; somewhat acid to neutral soil; if there is a lack of rainfall before the plant starts to flower, no additional feeding necessary; sow in spring, from seeds of the previous year, in rows 12in (30cm) apart in protected locations (indoors) starting in February.

Companion planting: with annuals and perennials that grow less vigorously.

Arnica.

Southernwood.

Harvesting: Flowers starting in June; roots starting in September for drying.

Medicinal: Inhibits infections; supports wound healing; has antirheumatism properties; externally, use only as a salve for bruises, sprains, inflammation, and insect bites. *Some people are hypersensitive to this herb.*

Cosmetic: Helps healing process for blemished skin; improves circulation; used for hair treatment (see page 74).

Southernwood
Artemisia abrotanum
Compositae

Southernwood strengthens the stomach, but only use it in very small amounts because of its sharp, bitter aroma.

Characteristics: Perennial semishrub; grows up to 40in (1m) tall; yellow-white flowers from August through September; has a spicy, lemony scent.

Active Substances: Essential oils, bitters, and tannic acid.

Cultivation: Sunny to partly shady locations; prefers dry, humus soil containing lime; propagate from division and cuttings, plant in spring 16 × 16in (40 × 40cm) apart in wind-protected location; will grow in containers.

Harvest: Fresh tip of shoots beginning in spring; from a healthy plant, tea from flowers July and August; store dried leaves in glass containers.

Culinary: Add fresh or dried tips of shoots in small amounts to salads, cottage cheese, sauces, and fish.

Medicinal: Strengthens stomach; supports digestion (in carefully chosen doses).

Wormwood
Artemisia absinthium
Compositae

This plant has a strong scent and a bitter taste.

Wormwood

Characteristics: Perennial; grows up to 5ft (1.5m) tall; yellow flowers from July into September in the northern hemisphere.

Active Substances: Essential oils, bitters, and tannic acid. Can be poisonous and addictive if used excessively.

Cultivation: Sunny to partially shady locations; undemanding of soil conditions and care; cut back once a year; plant 16 × 16in (40 × 40cm) apart; propagate by cuttings, division (spring and fall), or seeding in spring.

Don't plant wormwood in the vicinity of fennel. It does well with others of the Compositae and Liliaceae families and, with sufficient distance between them, with other plants.

Harvesting: Fresh, young shoots and leaves May into late fall; for teas, harvest before plant begins to bloom.

Medicinal: Increases appetite; use as a stomach and gallbladder tea. *Do not use this herb during pregnancy. Never use in large amounts.*

Tarragon
Artemisia dracunculus
Compositae

When buying tarragon, insist on German tarragon (*A. dracunculus* var. *sativa*), not the Russian variety. The aroma of the former is superior!

Characteristics: Perennial; grows up to 5ft (1.5m) tall; whitish green, inconspicuous flowers starting in July; has a spicy fragrance.

Active Substances: Essential oils, tannic acid, and bitter substances.

Cultivation: Sunny, but partly shady locations if enough moisture present and if protected during winter months; propagate German tarragon through division and runners, grow the Russian variety from seeds in rows 12–16in (30–40cm) apart in spring.

Companion planting: works well with cucumbers.

Harvesting: Tips from fresh shoots May until late fall; for drying and freezing purposes, before plant goes into bloom.

Tarragon

Mugwort.

Winter cress.

Culinary: Always best when used fresh in soups, salads, sauces, with fowl, cottage cheese, in spirits and wines, herbal vinegar, and when making mustard; can boil.

Medicinal: Improves digestion and gallbladder; increases appetite; is a diuretic.

Mugwort
Artemisia vulgaris
Compositae

Mugwort is an undemanding herb.

Characteristics: Perennial; grows up to 6½ft (2m) tall; small, yellow, ball-shaped flowers June through September; fresh, spicy fragrance.

Active Substances: Essential oils with cineole and bitter substances.

Cultivation: Undemanding of climate and soil; prefers sunny locations; propagate through division, cuttings, and from seeds in spring.

Companion planting: does well with cabbage and kohlrabi.

Harvesting: Fresh leaves and young shoots for seasoning before going into bloom; collect flower spikes just before flowering, dry without leaves.

Culinary: Fresh or dried with roasts, fowl, lamb, and vegetables; can include when cooking.

Medicinal: As tea, reduces digestive problems; improves appetite.

Winter Cress
Barbarea vulgaris
Cruciferae

Sometimes people call this herb yellow rocket.

Characteristics: Biennial; grows up to 24in (60cm) tall; bright yellow flowers in the second year, starting in April in the northern hemisphere; faint fragrance; taste similar to cress.

Active Substances: Essential oils and vitamin C.

Cultivation: Sunny, but also partially shady locations; moist, loamy soil; assure even moisture; mulch with organic material; propagate in spring or fall with seeds.

Companion planting: does well with all other herbs.

Harvesting: Fresh shoots and leaves throughout year, particularly during winter months; use only when fresh.

Culinary: Use for cress salads and as addition to other salads, raw vegetables, in herb butter, and in bouillon; can also steam.

Medicinal: Increases appetite; cleanses blood; is a diuretic; helps heal wounds.

Borage produces a perfect bee pasture!

Borage
Borago officinalis
Boraginaceae

Characteristics: Annual; grows up to 32in (80cm) tall; blue, but also pink and white, star-shaped flowers arranged in loose corollas, from June through September; spicy fragrance with a hint of cucumber.

Active Substances: Mucilage, saponin, and tannic acid.

Cultivation: Sunny to partly shady locations; nutrient-rich soil; keep soil moderately moist; if fed with compost, no additional fertilizing necessary; sow seeds beginning in April in rows 10in (25cm) apart; use consecutive planting, but borage seeds itself easily; seeds need darkness to germinate; does well in containers.

Companion planting: cucumbers, cabbages, kohlrabi, beets, celery, tomatoes, and zucchini.

Harvesting: Young leaves and flowers May through October; use only fresh or frozen.

Culinary: Freshly cut, add to cucumber and other salads; finely chopped in green sauces (see page 65); with fish, eggs, potatoes, cottage cheese, mushrooms, juices, apple wine, beer; flowers are edible and are wonderful as a garnish.

Medicinal: As tea, cleanses blood; is a diuretic; promotes perspiration; used in cases of arthritis and infections of the respiratory tract.

Cosmetic: Refreshes tired skin.

Marigold
Calendula officinalis
Compositae

From June through November, marigolds have yellow and orange flowers that open up in the morning and close again in the evening (see photo, page 94).

Yellow and orange marigolds ready for harvesting. Lighter ones are past harvesting.

Characteristics: Annual; grows up to 20in (50cm) tall.

Active Substances: Essential oils, flavonoid, and carotenoid.

Cultivation: Sunny locations; average, well-drained soil; sow seeds from March on in rows 12in (30cm) apart, thin later, leaving 12in (30cm) between plants; self-seeding possible.

Companion planting: peas, cucumbers, asparagus, cabbage, kohlrabi, carrots, tomatoes. Good protection against nematodes; replenishes worn-out soil.

Harvesting: Flowers after they open, June through November.

Culinary: Single flower may substitute for saffron as food coloring.

Medicinal: As mouthwash, relieves inflamed gums and throat; use as compress for sprains; as addition to salves (see page 75) for poorly healing wounds and minor injuries. Add to teas in small amounts to give color.

Cosmetic: To treat rough, cracked, and inflamed skin.

Peppers
Capsicum annum
Solanaceae

The fruit of pepper plants come in a variety of sizes and shapes and range in color from green to yellow, orange, and red.

Characteristics: Annual; grows up to 20 inches (50 cm) tall; yellowish white flowers from June through fall.

Active Substances: Alkaloid capsaicin (very hot), sugar, minerals, and vitamins C, A, B_1, and B_2.

Cultivation: Protected, warm, and sunny locations; humus soil; water regularly; generous feeding with compost or compost tea (see page 29); start seeds indoors; plant in garden 16 × 16in (40 × 40cm) apart in May; most varieties need support from stakes; mulching increases yield; very sensitive to frost; will grow in containers.

Red peppers.

Chilies, also a type of paprika.

Companion planting: does well with cucumbers, kohlrabi, and tomatoes; less well with bush and pole beans.

Harvesting: In August when fruits are completely ripe; in fall when danger of frost; can pick when not quite ripe.

Culinary: As a vegetable and to season meat, soups, and sauces; dried and ground, fresh, or pickled.

Caraway
Carum carvi
Umbelliferae

Caraway is an undemanding herb.
Characteristics: Biennial; grows up to 40in (1m) tall; flowers and seed formation in the second year, May and June; white and pink flowers in compound umbells; individual fruit carries two seeds each.

Cross caraway (*Cuminum cyminum*), seldom grown, has a much stronger aroma than regular caraway.

Active Substances: Essential oils with limonene and flavonoid.
Cultivation: Sunny locations if possible; prefers humid climate, fertile, deep

Yellow paprika.

Caraway in bloom.

soil; in mountain regions, protect during the winter months; seed in rows 14 inches (35cm) apart in July and August.

Caraway plants should be this healthy as winter approaches, assuring that very little frost damage will occur.

Caraway seed pods.

Companion planting: does well with bush and pole beans, peas, cucumbers, potatoes, cabbage, kohlrabi, lettuce, beets, and spinach; less well with chives (increased danger of caraway-moth infection).

Harvesting: Branches with seed pods starting in July, early in the morning when seeds turn brown; bundle and hang up to dry.

Culinary: Seeds for cabbage, sauerkraut, one-dish meals, salads, meat, cold cuts, cottage cheese, cheeses, baked goods, and spirits.

Medicinal: Reduces flatulence and loss of appetite; relieves cramps.

Centaury
Centaurium erythraea
Gentianaceae

Characteristics: Annual or biennial; grows up to 20in (50cm) tall; blooms from June through September in the northern hemisphere.

Active Substances: Bitters and flavonoid.

Cultivation: Sunny to partly shady locations; humus-rich soil; water during dry periods; sow seeds in spring in rows in carefully prepared beds (see page 21); best results from seedlings started indoors; plant seedlings 6 × 8in (15 × 20cm) apart.

Harvesting: When in bloom; dry roots for teas.

Culinary: Add to herbal wines and spirits.

Medicinal: As tea, stimulates appetite, aids indigestion, flatulence, and poor metabolism; *do not use in cases of stomach or intestinal ulcers.*

Centaury.

Roman Chamomile
Chamaemelum nobile (Anthemis nobilis)
Compositae

Characteristics: Perennial; grows up to 10in (25cm) tall; flowers from June to September in the northern hemisphere; fragrant plant.
Active Substances: Essential oils, bitters, and flavonoid.
Cultivation: Sunny to partially shady locations; grows in any type of soil; grows well as fragrant ground cover (see page 36); can mow with high lawn mower setting; spread seeds in spring; propagate by division,

plant 8 × 8in (20 × 20cm) apart; will grow in containers.
Harvesting: Pick fresh flowers while in bloom; store in glass containers.
Culinary: Fresh flowers add aroma to aperitifs.
Medicinal: Is anti-inflammatory, anti-spasmodic, similar to German chamomile (see page 98); improves appetite; is an antiflatulent; use as mouthwash.
Cosmetic: For the treatment of sensitive, dry skin; lotion for blond hair.

German Chamomile
*Chamomilla recutita
(Matricaria chamomilla)*
Compositae

German chamomile has a cone-shaped empty space at the base of the flower.
Characteristics: Annual; grows up to 20in (50cm) tall; starts blooming in May; intense fragrance.
Active Substances: Essential oils with flavonoid.
Cultivation: Sunny locations, prefers loamy, humus-rich soil; sow seeds in

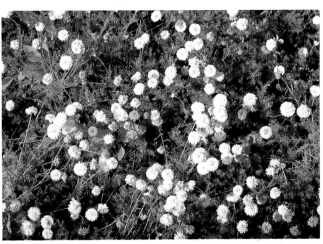

Roman chamomile.

German chamomile.

spring in rows 8in (20cm) apart; can also grow in containers.

Companion planting: does well with cabbage, kohlrabi, leeks, radishes, horseradish, celery, and onions.

Harvesting: In general, flowers with short stems or branches with flowers for drying during dry weather; store dried flowers in glass containers.

Medicinal: Is anti-inflammatory and antibacterial; helps heal wounds; use as an antispasmodic; for stomach and intestinal problems, mouth and throat infections; use as mouthwash, for compresses, the bath; use for inhalation; home remedy for toothaches.

Cosmetics: Hair treatment for blond hair and hair loss; tolerated by every type of skin, particularly effective for sensitive, dry skin; used as facial lotion, facial steam bath, facial masks, and in creams.

Scurvy Grass
Cochlearia officinalis
Cruciferae

Scurvy grass is a salt-loving plant growing by the shore. Mariners took it on voyages to treat scurvy.

Characteristics: Biennial; grows up to 12in (30cm) tall; in the first year, lower leaves are spoon-shaped; starting in May of the second year, white, fragrant flowers in racemes on leafy stems; leaves have a strong cress flavor and are salty and bitter.

Active Substances: Essential oils, vitamin C, and tannic acid.

Cultivation: Tolerates almost any location; needs moist, humus-rich soil; no additional feeding neces-

Scurvy grass.

sary if compost and mulch added initially; sow seeds in March and April or August and September in flat grooves, thin out to about 8in (20cm) apart.

Companion planting: does well with mustard and almost all vegetables except cabbage.

Harvest: Fresh leaves starting in summer from seeds sown early in spring; otherwise, in fall and winter until begins to bloom; use only fresh.

Culinary: For salads, potatoes, toppings; reduce the spicy flavor by using with chives.

Medicinal: Supports metabolic processes and digestion; cleanses blood; reduces skin problems; suited for use in salads and raw vegetable meals during spring cleansing.

Scurvy weed has white, fragrant flowers and starts blooming in June.

Coriander has an unpleasant scent.

Coriander
Coriandrum sativum
Umbelliferae

Characteristics: Annual; grows up to 28 inches (70cm) tall; white-pink flowers in July and August; fruit usually does not fall apart; when dried, has a very pleasant aroma.

Active Substances: Essential oils with linalool and geraniol.

Cultivation: Sunny, warm locations; sandy, humus-rich soil; sow seeds in rows about 12in (30cm) apart; young plants need a considerable amount of water.

When fresh, coriander pods are smooth.

Companion planting: cucumbers, potatoes, cabbage, kohlrabi, and beets.

Harvest: When roots die off and turn brown (usually starting in August); cut plants early in morning and allow to dry in sun on towels or tied into bundles and hung upside down; store seeds in glass jars or tin cans.

Dried coriander seeds.

Culinary: Young, freshly cut herbs as flavoring for salads and sauces; aromatic spice used in baking to preserve food; for game, fish, beef stews, cold cuts, sauces, raw vegetable dishes, and beets.
Medicinal: Stimulates appetite; aids digestion; is an antiflatulent; use as tonic in case of stomach and intestinal problems.

Dragonhead
Dracocephalum moldavica
Labiatae

Dragonhead, also called Turkish balm, is a valuable plant for bees.
Characteristics: Annual; grows up to 24in (60cm) tall; blue-violet flowers from June till August; has a lemon-balm fragrance.
Active Substances: Essential oils, flavonoid, bitters, and tannic acid.
Cultivation: Sunny locations; humus-rich soil; needs sufficient watering but should not sit in water; for best yield,

Dragonhead.

Medicinal: Similar to lemon balm; as tea, reduces nervous stomach, intestinal problems, headaches, insomnia; improves digestion.

Rocket Cress
Eruca sativa
Cruciferae

Characteristics: Annual; grows up to 20in (50cm) tall; light yellow flowers starting in May; very fragrant.

Active Substances: Essential oils, minerals, and vitamins A and C.

Cultivation: Undemanding of location and soil conditions; watering during dry periods increases yield; sow seeds in spring in rows 8in (20cm) apart; reseed monthly for continuous harvest; will grow in containers.

feed with compost or compost teas; sow seeds in rows in the spring; also suitable for growing in containers.

Companion planting: as far as is known, compatible with all annual herbs.

Harvesting: When flowers appear or when almost finished blooming, starting in July; store dry in glass jars.

Rocket cress, ready to harvest.

Rocket cress in bloom.

Active Substances: Essential oils with minerals and vitamins A, B, and C.
Cultivation: Watering necessary in the early stages and during long dry spells; compost feed and mulch during summer months; if necessary, additional organic surface feeding; sow seeds in spring in rows 16 inches (40cm) apart; will grow in containers.
Harvesting: Delicate leaves fresh all summer; cut seeds as soon as turn brown, hang upside down for storage.
Culinary: Fresh greens for seasoning soups, sauces, salad dressings, and fish dishes; seeds for baking and spirits.
Medicinal: Is an expectorate; relieves cramps; reduces flatulence; as tea, recommended for children's stomach-aches.

Companion planting; similar to mustard.

Harvesting: Use only fresh leaves; during winter months, grow on windowsill.
Culinary: Similar to garden cress; gives zest to salads; with butter and cheese as topping; use leaves to decorate cold platters.
Medicinal: Cleanses blood; use as a tonic and stimulant.

Fennel
Foeniculum vulgare
Umbelliferae

Characteristics: Perennial; grows up to 6½ft (2m) tall; yellow flowers from June till October; has a spicy, sweet fragrance; long, carrotlike roots.

Fennel.

Cosmetic: Use as oil or lotion to soothe dry and rough skin.

Sweet woodruff.

Sweet Woodruff
Galium odoratum
Rubiaceae

This is a favorite ground cover under trees.

Characteristics: Perennial; grows up to 28in (70cm) tall; fragrant, white flowers starting in May; distributes strong, typical fragrance when plant begins to dry.

Active Substances: Glycosides, tannic acid, and bitters.

Cultivation: Shady locations; loose and moist, humus-rich soil; sow seed in fall (frost germination); propagate through division; after plant establishes itself, it propagates automatically.

Harvesting: From second year on, remove flowers; use when wilted or after dried for tea.

Culinary: Wilted herb to give aroma to fruit punch, fruit salads, and apple jelly; also used for its fragrance in potpourris.

Medicinal: Relief for cramps; is calmative; relieves nervousness and insomnia; gives aroma to teas. *Use with care: Dangerous if used too much.*

St.-John's-Wort
Hypericum perforatum
Guttiferae

Characteristics: Perennial; grows to 32in (80cm) tall; golden yellow flowers from June till September; flowers release red substances when squeezed (see photo, page 104).

Active Substances: Essential oils, tannic acid, and flavonoid.

Cultivation: Sunny locations; humus, but heavy soil, not too wet; sow seeds in fall, indoor sowing is advantageous; additional watering usually not necessary; feed with compost during summer; if necessary, feed with organic fertilizer; mulch if the soil is poor.

St.-John's-wort in bloom.

Companion planting: does well with all perennial plants.

Harvesting: Starting in June, flowering shoot tips for drying (for tea); fresh leaves and flowers for herbal oils.
Medicinal: As tea, for relief of anxiety, insomnia, minor depression, nerve pain, and rheumatism.
Cosmetic: Oil (for preparation see page 75) for homemade facial milk; cleanses, heals, and refreshes blemished and slightly inflamed skin.

Hyssop
Hyssopus officinalis
Labiatae

A decorative semi-shrub; hyssop attracts beneficial insects.
Characteristics: Grows up to 20in (50cm) tall; lively blue-violet, less often pink or white flowers, starting in July; strong fragrance; sharp and bitter taste.
Active substances: Essential oils, glycoside, and tannic acid.
Cultivation: Full sun; warm, lime-rich humus soil; propagate by division, seedlings, and seeds; plant 12 × 12in (30 × 30cm) apart; will grow in containers.

Companion planting: with all perennial herbs.

Harvesting: Fresh until plant goes into bloom;

Hyssop does well in pots.

Hyssop starts to produce violet-blue flowers in July.

Elecampane in the garden.

used directly as spice; just prior to the opening of the flower, dry for use during winter.

Culinary: Fresh or dried for potato dishes, legume recipes, soups, meat, one-pot dishes, and herbal wine.

Medicinal: Supports digestion; relieves cramps; use for coughs; is a stimulant.

Elecampane
Inula helenium
Compositae

Elecampane is a honey plant.

Characteristics: Perennial; grows up to 6½ft (2m) tall; roots grow deep into the soil; bright, yellow, small flowers that look like miniature sunflowers from June to September in the northern hemisphere.

Active Substances: Inulin and essential oils with bitters.

Cultivation: Sunny locations; nutrient-rich, heavy soil; water during first season when necessary; feed with compost and mulch during summer; propagate by dividing the root stock; plant in spring or fall 20 × 20in (50 × 50cm) apart.

Companion planting: with all tall, perennial plants.

Elecampane in bloom.

Harvesting: Roots starting in the second year in fall: clean, chop, and dry at 95°F (35°C).
Medicinal: Is an expectorant; recommended for bronchitis and coughs; stimulates digestion and kidney activities; *poisonous in larger amounts; may create allergic reactions.*
Cosmetic: As poultice or compress for blemished skin and acne.

Bay
Laurus nobilis
Lauraceae

Characteristics: Perennial; grows up to 65ft (20m) tall as a tree or shrub; evergreen, not frost-hardy; yellow-white flowers starting in May; berries are black, egg-shaped, size of a cherry; leaves have an aromatic, spicy scent.
Active Substances: Essential oils with bitters and tannic acid.
Cultivation: Water regularly (except during winter); give repeated feedings with compost tea (see page 29); keep plant in frost-free place during winter; propagate with cuttings; will grow in containers.
Harvesting: Leaves that are year old and young shoots for fresh use or for drying.
Culinary: For fish and meat marinades, soups, sauces, and to flavor vinegar; also used as part of a bouquet garni.
Medicinal: Stimulates appetite and digestion; bay oil from the berries used externally to increase circulation; is an antirheumatic lotion.
Cosmetic: Bay-oil packs strengthen and regenerate hair.

Bay.

Lavender
Lavandula angustifolia
Labiatae

Lavender works well as a border and in small hedges.

Characteristics: Perennial semi-shrub; grows up to 24in (60cm) tall; small silver-grey–green leaves; starting in July, fragrant, blue flowers on long stems.

Active Substances: Essential oils, tannic acid, and bitters.

Cultivation: Full sun; lime- and humus-rich soil; do not let stand in wet soil; water during dry periods; add compost, mulch, and organic fertilizer until August; propagate through cuttings; seed in spring in rows 12 × 12in (30 × 30cm) apart; after blooming, cut green back slightly; will grow in containers.

Lavender.

Companion planting: does well with all perennial herbs that grow up to 20in (50cm) at maturity.

Harvesting: Young shoots and fresh leaves for seasoning, starting in May; right after flowers open, cut and tie together and hang upside down to dry; do same with flowering branches.

Culinary: Fresh green for seasoning sauces, one-pot meals, and fish (add while food is cooking); dried flowers for fragrant pillows and spirits.

Medicinal: As tonic, promotes sleep; is an antiflatulent; stimulates gallbladder activity; to relieve rheumatic symptoms, rub lavender spirits into affected areas.

Cosmetic: Add to bathwater for calming effect; for treatment of blemished skin; used for compresses and in shampoo.

Motherwort
Leonurus cardiaca
Labiatae

These plants attract bees (photo, see page 108).

Characteristics: Perennial; grows up to 48in (1.2m) tall; pink to red flowers from June till September.

Motherwort, a wonderful plant for the "farmer's garden."

Garden Cress
Lepidium sativum
Cruciferae

Newer varieties with larger leaves bring greater yields. Cress is an excellent example of a fast-growing indoor plant (see page 55).

Characteristics: Annual; grows up to 20in (50cm) tall; white, rarely reddish flowers; reddish brown seeds encapsulated in small pods; flowering depends on when sown, from May to late fall; radishlike, hot, spicy taste.

Active Substances: Mustard-oil glycoside and vitamins A and C.

Cultivation: Sunny as well as partly shady locations; undemanding, but needs to be constantly moist; sow seeds in rows 6in (15cm) apart; germi-

Active Substances: Bitters, glycoside, alkaloid, traces of essential oils, flavonoid, and tannic acid.

Cultivation: Robust plant; sunny location with sufficient room; plant at least 16–20in (40–50cm) apart; nutrient-rich soil; cut back in fall; sow seeds in spring.

Harvesting: Flowering tip of shoots; dried for teas; several harvests possible during season.

Medicinal: As tonic, improves nervous heartbeats; relieves migraine headaches; helps poor digestion; similar in effect to valerian. *Do not use during pregnancy.*

Motherwort in bloom.

nates and grows rather quickly; therefore, repeat sowing often; will grow in containers.

Companion planting: with radishes, horseradish, and lettuce.

Harvesting: Use only fresh and as seasoning herb; white flowers are edible and even spicier than leaves.

Culinary: For salads, green sauce (see page 65), cottage cheese, egg dishes, potatoes, raw vegetables, and toppings.

Medicinal: Stimulates appetite and digestion; cleanses blood; is a diuretic; use as a spice during spring cleansing.

Garden cress ready for harvest.

Broad-leaved garden cress.

Overripe garden cress.

Lovage
Levisticum officinale
Umbelliferae

The whole plant has a strong celery scent.

Characteristics: Perennial; when in bloom, grows up to 6½ft (2m) tall; faint yellow flowers; thick, intertwined roots.
Active Substances: Essential oils, tannic acid, and vitamin C.
Cultivation: Sunny to partly shady locations; moist, nutrient-rich soil and sufficient space; watering is necessary during prolonged dry period in first year; propagate by division of the root stock; sow seed in spring in rows 12–16in (30–40cm) apart; in spring, apply compost when turning the soil over and mulch; will grow in containers.
Harvesting: Continuous cutting of young leaves for seasoning; drying beginning in June or July, cutting back vigorously; roots in fall or early in spring.
Culinary: Fresh herb (also dried and frozen) for soups, one-pot dishes, sauces, fish, and meat dishes; young stems boiled in sugar as candy; very spicy, use in moderation; roots are particularly aromatic; cook together with food.
Medicinal: Stimulates digestion; is an antiflatulent and a diuretic; *do not use in case of kidney disease or during pregnancy.*

Lovage.

Flax
Linum usitatissimum
Linaceae

Flax seeds are a laxative.
Characteristics: Annual; grows up to 40in (1m) tall; light blue flowers starting in July or August; flat, brown or yellow seeds in pea-size pods.
Active Substances: Mucilage, fixed oil, glycosides, pectin, and vitamin F.
Cultivation: Full sun; soil in good condition with a pH value of 6.0; additional watering and feeding usually necessary; sow seeds in rows 8in (20cm) apart as soon as possible in March to assure sufficient growing time for a worthwhile harvest.

Harvesting: As soon as seeds in pods rustle; allow pods to dry before threshing.
Culinary: For baking; can use seeds whole or ground up.
Medicine: Is a laxative and a diuretic; for weak intestine, use 1 teaspoon (5ml) flaxseeds in the morning and evening with meals, making sure to drink plenty of liquids; boil seeds as poultices for rheumatism.
Cosmetic: A flaxseed poultice allows skin to absorb moisture and creams; masks for dry skin.

Flax.

Wild mallow.

Common Mallow or Wild Mallow
Malva sylvestris
Malvaceae

Characteristics: Perennial; grows up to 40in (1m) tall; pink-violet flower from June till September in the northern hemisphere.
Active Substances: Mucilage, glycoside, and tannic acid.
Cultivation: Sunny locations, otherwise undemanding; if necessary, water in first year; sow seeds in spring in rows 16in (40cm) apart, thin later.
Harvesting: As soon as plant starts to bloom, pick flowers and leaves for teas; roots in spring and fall; store dried herb· in glass jars.
Culinary: Young leaves for salad.

Medicinal: As a tea, soothes irritation; is anti-inflammatory; relieves stomach and intestinal problems; will reduce coughs; as mouthwash and to gargle.

Cosmetic: Used as compress for irritated skin.

Horehound
Marrubium vulgare
Labiatae

Characteristics: Perennial; grows up to 24in (60cm) tall; from June to September in the northern hemisphere, producing small, white flowers.

Active Substances: Bitters, tannic acid, and essential oil.

Cultivation: No special requirements; in the wild, prefers sunny, dry locations and lime-containing soil; sow seeds in spring.

Horehound has a scent reminiscent of apples.

Companion planting: does well with all types of perennial herbs of equal height.

Harvesting: Leaves and shoots until in full bloom; for teas, store dried as any other herb.

Medicinal: As a tea, reduces coughs, gallbladder and liver problems.

Lemon Balm
Melissa officinalis
Labiatae

This herb has a strong lemony scent which evaporates very quickly if stored improperly.

Characteristics: Perennial; grows up to 40in (1m) tall; lemony scent; white to bluish flowers from July till October in the northern hemisphere.

Active Substances: Essential oil with citral, linalool, geraniol, flavonoid, and tannic acid.

Cultivation: Warm, protected locations; sandy soil; water only during first year and during dry periods; use organic fertilizer and mulch; protect in colder regions; propagate through division of large root stocks; sow seeds from April in rows 12in (30cm) apart; will grow in containers.

Lemon balm in bloom.

Lemon balm without flowers.

Companion planting: works well with cabbage.

Harvesting: From spring to late fall, young shoots and leaves fresh as seasoning; from end of June, just before blooming, strip leaves from shoots and dry in thin layers to preserve color; store lemon balm just like any other herb; preserve by drying and freezing.

Culinary: Fresh leaves for salads, soups, sauces, cottage cheese, mushrooms, meat, fish, fowl, and game; add at end; don't boil.

Medicine: As tea and in spirits, has sedative properties; relieves cramps, insomnia, nervous headaches, and stomach and intestinal problems.

Cosmetic: Used as soothing facial compress for oily skin; rejuvenates and tightens skin; is relaxing when added to the bath.

Mints
Mentha
Labiatae

All plants in the mint family have strong scents, grow vigorously, and propagate by runners.

Characteristics: Perennial; grow up to 16–32in (40–80cm) tall; all varieties strongly aromatic (see photo, page 114).

Active Substances: Essential oils with menthol, cineole, tannic acid, and flavonoid.

Apple mint.

Companion planting: potatoes, cabbage, kohlrabi, lettuce, carrots, and tomatoes.

Harvesting: Young shoot and leaves spring to fall; fresh for seasoning and teas; for drying, place on a flat surface in two to three layers before onset of blooming.

Culinary: Fresh for salads, sauces, soups, raw vegetables, eggs, cottage cheese, jellies, drinks, herbal vinegar, wine, and to add flavor.

Medicinal: Relieves pain, of stomach and intestinal problems; reduces nausea; improves minor colic; supports liver and gallbladder function; rub a few drops of peppermint oil (see page 68) on skin for joint pain.

Mentha crispa: Curly mint
Mentha × piperita: Peppermint with violet, pink, or white flowers
Mentha × piperita var. *citrata:* Orange mint
Mentha spicata: Spearmint
Mentha suaveolens: Apple mint
Mentha suaveolens 'Bowles': Pineapple mint

Cultivation: Sunny to partially shady locations; moist, humus-rich soil; propagate by runners; plant parts and cuttings in spring 8 × 12in (20 × 30cm) apart; cut back vigorously when attacked by mint rust; does well in containers.

Curly mint.

Cosmetic: Facial steam bath for blemished, oily skin with large pores; refreshes and disinfects; for the sauna.

Broad-leaved Spignel or Baldmony
Meum athamanticum
Umbelliferae

Characteristics: Perennial; grows up to 20in (50cm) tall; white, less often reddish, umbels from June to August; strong root stock; intensely spicy aroma.
Active Substances: Essential oils and minerals.
Cultivation: Sunny to partially shady locations; moist, nutrient-rich soil;

Peppermint.

Spignel.

very sensitive to lime, therefore, do not plant in freshly limed areas; remove flower buds for increased yield in leaves; water first year during dry periods; mulch and feed with compost; propagate through seeds and division in spring.
Harvesting: Fresh greens throughout summer as seasoning; stems with flowers for dry arrangements; collect seeds in September and roots in late fall.
Culinary: Fresh greens add sweet aroma for seasoning (see page 110); seeds and roots for spirits.
Medicinal: Increases appetite; supports digestion, especially in the form of root tea.

Bergamot, long used by the Native American Oswego people, soon became known to early American settlers as Oswego Tea.

Bergamot or Oswego Tea
Monarda didyma
Labiatae

Bees love this!
Characteristics: Perennial; grows up to 40in (1m) tall; leaves have a lemony aroma; red flowers; blooms from June to October in the northern hemisphere.

> The *Monarda citrodora,* lemon bergamot, is an extraordinarily aromatic plant for the garden.

Active Substances: Essential oils with tannic acid, bitters, and minerals.
Cultivation: Sunny locations, otherwise undemanding; sow seeds in spring in rows 12in (30cm) apart; propagate by division of the root ball and cuttings; remove wilted flowers; must cut back

every year; watering necessary during dry periods; mulching essential to keep plant from overgrowing; usually not planted together with other plants.
Harvesting: Fresh leaves all summer; leaves, flowers, and flowering branches June and July to dry for teas and cold drinks.
Culinary: To give aroma to fruit salads, jams, marmalades, etc.
Medicinal: As tea, relieves indigestion; improves the taste of medicinal preparations.

Watercress
Nasturtium officinale
Cruciferae

Characteristics: Perennial; grows up to 32 inches (80 cm) tall; ¾in (2cm) white racemes from May through September; sausage-shaped pods.
Active Substances: Mustard-oil glycosides, bitters, minerals, vitamins A, B_2,

Watercress.

Watercress in bloom.

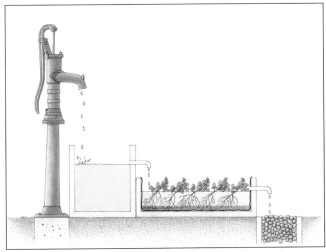

Growing watercress in a trough: Watercress does exceedingly well in a trough or swamp bed. A constant supply of flowing water comes from a water container placed under a faucet (left). Water runs off onto a gravel bed located at the end of the trough (right).

C, and E.

Cultivation: In shallow places or containers that allow water to flow through; a container under a dripping faucet also works; sow seeds in June; propagate through shoot cuttings; winter-hardy to 14°F (−10°C).

Harvesting: Fresh shoots October till May; collect seeds starting in September; only use shoots when fresh; dry and store seeds in glass jars.

Culinary: Green shoots for salads, toppings, meat dishes; add seeds to meat dishes and salads as seasoning; tastes like radishes.

Medicinal: Cleanses blood; regulates metabolism; is a diuretic; relieves rheumatism and acne.

Cosmetic: Cleanses skin (blackheads); bleaches freckles; good treatment for oily hair (as a rinse after shampooing).

Catnip
Nepeta cataria
Labiatae

Cats love catnip.

Characteristics: Perennial; grows up to 40in (1m) tall; blooms from June to September; intense mintlike fragrance; bitter, sharp taste.

Active Substances: Essential oils.

Catnip.

A toy mouse is a favorite plaything for a cat, especially when stuffed with dried catnip and a bit of valerian root.

Cultivation: Sunny, dry locations; sandy soil; undemanding; watering usually not necessary; fertilize with compost and mulch in spring; sow seeds in rows 12 × 12in (30 × 30cm) apart in spring; propagate by division and cuttings; will grow in containers.

Harvesting: Cuttings several times during year; dry leaves and give to cats to play with (see drawing on left).

Medicine: Relieves cramps; is a stomach tonic; occasionally used for coughs and diarrhea.

Basil
Ocimum basilicum
Labiatae

Basil becomes a bee pasture!

Characteristics: Annual; grows up to 24in (60cm) tall; rich in nectar; yellow flowers from June to September; spicy fragrance comes in several different varieties: large leaves, small leaves, and different-colored leaves; sensitive to cold.

Active Substances: Essential oils with linalool, cineole, and tannic acid.

Cultivation: Sunny, protected locations; humus, warm soil; sufficient wa-

Basil.

ter; protect from wind; fertilize as needed with compost and organic fertilizer, also compost teas and brews (see page 29).

Companion planting: works well with cucumbers, fennel, salsify root, tomatoes, zucchini, onions.

Sow seeds in spring in rows 10in (25cm) apart, consecutive sowing throughout warm season; start seedlings indoors; will grow in containers.

Basil in bloom.

Harvesting: Leaves and young shoots fresh throughout summer; for drying and freezing, cut before plant goes into bloom.

Culinary: With meat, fish, vegetables, one-pot dishes, soups, salads, raw vegetables; do not boil.
Medicinal: Stimulates appetite and digestion; tonic for the digestive system, including flatulence; is a diuretic; relieves cramps.

Sweet marjoram.

Sweet Marjoram
Origanum majorana
Labiatae

Sweet marjoram is the gentlest and mildest of the varieties.
Characteristics: Annual; grows up to 20in (50cm) tall; white or pinkish red flowers from July to October; spicy fragrance.
Active Substances: Essential oils, bitters, and tannic acid.

Cultivation: Sunny locations; loose, humus-rich soil; water during dry periods; sensitive to fungus when soil remains wet; apply mulch in summer; feed with compost; sow seeds in rows in spring; cover small seeds lightly with soil or sand; thin young plants to 4–6in (10–15cm) apart; does well in containers.

Companion planting: carrots and onions.

Harvesting: Fresh herb when needed for seasoning; for use during winter, harvest leaves before onset of blooming; possible to get three harvests out of each plant; leaves can remain on twigs, dried and stored.

Culinary: Fresh or dried for hearty potato and meat dishes, one-pot dishes, tomatoes, and cottage cheese; add at end when dish is almost ready.

Medicine: Stimulates appetite; relieves indigestion with cramps and flatulence; lessens cold symptoms.

Cosmetic: Add to bath to relax muscles.

Oregano or Wild Marjoram
Origanum vulgare
Labiatae

Oregano produces a bee pasture!

Characteristics: Perennial; grows up to 20in (50cm) tall; pink, red, or white flowers from July to September; very aromatic.

Active Substances: Essential oils with thymol, carvacrol, tannic acid, bitters, and vitamin C.

Cultivation: Sunny locations; humus-rich, warm, dry soil; mulching beneficial; sow seeds in spring in rows 10in (25cm) apart; propagate by cuttings or division; cut back several times a year; grows well in containers.

Harvesting: Fresh, young shoots from spring to beginning of winter; harvest in full bloom to dry for use as tea and as spice.

Culinary: Fresh or dried with fish, meat, spaghetti, pizza, tomatoes, sauces, and potato dishes.

Medicine: Stimulates appetite; aids digestion; relieves cramps; use as nerve tonic and in case of bladder trouble; relieves rheumatism.

Cosmetic: Add to water for a relaxing bath.

Oregano or wild marjoram.

Parsnip
Pastinaca sativa
Umbelliferae

When ground up, the plant releases a spicy aroma.
Characteristics: Annual; yellow flowers in the second year; meaty, thick roots.
Active Substances: Essential oils.
Cultivation: Sunny locations; nutrient-rich, deep soil; if needed, liquid feeding in August; sow seeds in March and April in rows 12in (30cm) apart.

Companion planting: does well with potatoes, lettuce, radishes, horseradish, beets, celery, spinach, and onions.

Harvesting: Harvest roots in fall; winter-hardy, however, store in sand in

Parsnip roots.

basement; only cut and use leaves in spring.
Culinary: Leaves and new shoots are an excellent vegetable; use roots in soups, one-pot dishes, and with beef.
Medicinal: Used as a vegetable on diets for stomach and intestinal problems; is a diuretic.

Parsley
Petroselinum crispum
Umbelliferae

Characteristics: Biennial; grows up to 12in (30cm) tall; yellowish green leaves in the summer of the second year; carrotlike roots; spicy aroma.

Parsnip.

Flat parsley.

Parsley roots.

Harvesting: Continuously for using fresh; always take leaves from the outside first; for use during winter months, harvest in late summer for drying, freezing, or to put up with salt.

Active Substances: Essential oils with minerals and vitamins A and C.

Cultivation: Sunny to partially shady locations; nutrient-rich soil; no fresh manure, instead use compost and liquid compost made from herbal brew; sow seeds starting in March because germination is very slow; sow together with radish or lettuce seeds (the latter germinate fast and finish before the parsley seeds come up); if growing in the garden is problematic, start seeds indoors; does well in containers.

Companion planting: does well with cucumbers, leeks, radishes, horseradish, tomatoes, and onions; does less well with head lettuce and chicory.

Curled parsley.

Culinary: For soups, sauces, meat dishes, cottage cheese, and vegetables; boiling destroys active substances.
Medicinal: Stimulates appetite; is a diuretetic; aids digestion; is a stimulant.
Cosmetic: Used to treat acne and freckles; soothing for inflamed skin; supports hair growth.

Anise
Pimpinella anisum
Umbelliferae

Characteristics: Annual; grows up to 32in (80cm) tall; small white or yellowish white flowers in June and July; pear-shaped, hairy fruits about 1–2in (3–5cm) long; sweet, aromatic fragrance.
Active Substances: Essential oils in the seeds.
Cultivation: Sunny, warm locations; humus-rich soil; watering usually not necessary; nitrogen-rich fertilizer delays ripening of seeds; sow seeds in early spring in rows 12in (30cm) apart.

Anise seeds.

Companion planting: in general, none recommended.

Harvesting: Seeds are ripe about six weeks after blooming; harvest seeds when brown, cut out main shoot, dry, and store.
Culinary: As seasoning for vegetables, salads, sauces, cottage cheese; seeds for baking, fruit compote, and homemade liquor.
Medicinal: Tea stimulates appetite, supports digestion, is an antiflatulent, and relieves cramps in cases of minor stomach problems; is an expectorant.

Large Variety Saxifrage or Great Burnet
Pimpinella major
Umbelliferae

Characteristics: Perennial; grows up to 32in (80cm) tall; white or pink flowers from June to August; thin roots have a hot and spicy taste, and smell like a farm animal.

Anise.

Large variety saxifrage or great burnet.

Harvesting: Roots in fall or spring; leaves almost all year round; use fresh; dry and store roots in glass jars.

Culinary: Young, sweet, spicy leaves for soups, sauces, and vegetables.

Medicinal: As tea (from roots), causes secretion of mucus and forces perspiration; is a diuretic; use for colds; stimulates kidney and liver activity; cleanses blood; use as mouthwash and throat wash.

Ribwort or English Plantain
Plantago lanceolata
Plantaginaceae

Other varieties of plantain, such as *P. major* and *P. media*, are less effective as medicinal plants and not grown as often.

Characteristics: Perennial; grows up to 16in (40cm) tall; yellow-white flowers from May to September.

Active Substances: Tannic acid, mucilage, glycoside, and vitamin C.

Cultivation: Sunny to partially shady locations; undemanding; water in early stages during dry periods; after cutting, feed with compost tea (see page 29) or herbal brew; sow seeds in rows 10in (25cm) apart at the end of March.

Although *Pimpinella saxifraga,* burnet saxifrage, a relative of *Pimpinella major,* has similar medicinal properties and usage, it is not as popular.

Active Substances: Essential oils, tannic acid, and saponin.

Cultivation: Sunny locations; deep soil; undemanding; feed with compost and organic fertilizer during dry periods in the first year; sow seeds beginning in March in rows 12in (30cm) apart.

Companion planting: with all slower-growing perennial herbs.

Companion planting: not usually done, but will do all right with all other herbs.

Ribwort.

Purslane.

Flowers of the ribwort.

Harvesting: Once or twice a year, always prior to the onset of flowers; dry and store leaves in glass jars.

Culinary: Young leaves for salads, raw vegetables, cottage cheese; as spinach-like vegetable dishes.

Medicinal: Has antibiotic properties; use for colds and bronchial problems and for inflammation of the mouth and throat area; relieves coughs and cramps; juices effective against coughs; externally for minor wounds and insect bites.

Cosmetic: Does well in cases of acne; relieves skin problems.

Purslane or Portulaca

Portulaca oleracea
Portulacaceae

This plant comes in several varieties.

Characteristics: Annual; grows up to 16in (40cm) tall; blooms from June to September in the northern hemisphere.

Active Substances: Vitamins A, B_1, and B_2, and minerals.

Cultivation: Sunny locations; light, humus-rich soil; sow seeds in rows 6in (15cm) apart beginning in May; don't cover seeds, simply moisten them; wa-

Purslane in bloom.

ter during dry periods; grows very fast; provide for several seedings; does well in containers.

Companion planting: does not do well near onions.

Harvesting: Only fresh leaves and shoots up to first frost.

English cowslip.

Culinary: Fresh for salads, raw vegetables, soups, vegetables, and meat dishes; freeze for use during winter months.
Medicinal: Cleanses blood; is a diuretic; stimulates digestion; juice from leaves and shoots relieves pain and inflammation from burns and heartburn.

English Cowslip
Primula veris
Primulaceae

American cowslip is a different plant, of the Buttercup family.
Characteristics: Annual; grows up to 10in (25cm) tall; yellow, bell-shaped flowers in April and May.
Active Substances: Saponin, tannic acid, flavonoid, essential oils, and glycoside.
Cultivation: Sunny locations; prefers lime-rich soil; add compost when preparing soil and mulching; sow seeds beginning in August and start indoors (cold germination), plant outside in May the following year 10 × 12in (25 × 30cm) apart; will grow in containers.

Companion planting: usually planted alone; does not do well when mixed with other plants.

Harvesting: Flower in second year for medicinal tea; roots for teas; store flowers and roots in a dry place.
Medicinal: As tea, is an expectorant and diuretic; tea for coughs, bronchitis, or colds.

Rosemary
Rosmarinus officinalis
Labiatae

This becomes a bee pasture!

Characteristics: Perennial semi-shrub; grows up to 28in (70cm) tall; light blue to violet flowers from March to August; spicy aroma.

Active Substances: Essential oils with cineole, camphor, flavonoid, bitters, and tannic acid.

Cultivation: Protected, sunny locations; lime-rich, warm, porous soil; water regularly in the first year, including several feedings with herbal brew or compost tea (see page 29); sow seeds indoors starting in April (need long time to germinate); plant outdoors in May; sensitive to frost; keep indoors in a bright room at 41°F (5°C); grows well in containers inside or on a balcony.

Rosemary.

Companion planting: does well with bush and pole beans and carrots; doesn't do well with cucumbers.

Harvesting: Young shoots throughout year; for drying, harvest leaves before and while still blooming.

Culinary: For meat, potatoes, and vegetable dishes; for grilling; boil with food; use in homemade wines and spirits.

Medicinal: Stimulates appetite; reduces overeating; relieves problems with stomach, intestines, and gallbladder; add to the bath for rheumatism; as herbal wine, improves circulation; not to be used in large amounts when pregnant.

Cosmetics: Use as herbal bath to improve circulation; rejuvenates tired skin; helps stop hair loss.

Rosemary in bloom.

Sorrel
Rumex rugosus
Polygonaceae

Characteristics: Perennial; grows up to 28in (70cm) tall; smooth, arrow-shaped, sour-tasting leaves; white-pink flowers from May till July.

Active Substances: Oxalic acid, vitamin C, minerals, bitters, and tannic acid.

Cultivation: Sunny to partly shady locations; moist, humus-rich, even loamy soil; feed with compost once a year; sow seeds starting March or April or in August or September in rows 10 inches (25cm) apart, thin out to 4–6in (10–15cm); break off flower stems; protect during winter and cover in spring to extend harvesting time; will grow in containers.

Sorrel.

Companion planting: suffers when in the vicinity of sorrel. Will grow with plants of the same height that are vigorous growers.

Harvesting: Fresh leaves continuously until winter; pick individual leaves and protect center growth.

Culinary: For salads, green sauce (see page 65), soups, and yogurt; as vegetable together with spinach.

Medicinal: Cleanses blood; improves appetite; *use sparingly, particularly for children and people with kidney problems.*

Cosmetic: Leaves and roots help blemished skin.

Rue
Ruta graveolens
Rutaceae

Characteristics: Perennial; grows up to 40in (1m) tall; yellow flowers beginning in June; spicy aroma, particularly on warm days.

Active Substances: Essential oils with glycoside.

Cultivation: Sunny locations; undemanding; yearly feeding with compost; sow seeds in rows starting April; also useful as small border; trim regularly; cut back once every year; in cold regions, protect during winter with twigs; will grow in containers.

Rue.

Low rue hedge.

Harvesting: Fresh, young shoots and leaves throughout year, including winter months.

Culinary: Fresh for meat and fish dishes, sauces, in herbal wine; always use sparingly; never boil.

Medicinal: Stimulates appetite; relieves cramps; is a diuretic; is calming.

Warning: Unhealthy in large amounts. Use only as seasoning; do not use during pregnancy.

Sage
Salvia officinalis
Labiatae

Characteristics: Semi-shrub; grows up to 28in (70cm) tall; light blue to violet flowers from May to August; intense, spicy fragrance.

Clary sage (*Salvia scarea*) is very spicy and even more fragrant than common sage. This variety is an attractive garden plant often grown for its fragrance.

Active Substances: Essential oils, flavonoid, bitters, and tannic acid.

Cultivation: Sunny locations; porous, preferably lime-rich soil; after harvesting, use liquid or organic fertilizer for strengthening; sow seeds in March in rows; propagate through runners; in colder climates, protect in winter; will grow in containers.

Sage in bloom.

Sage leaves.

Cosmetic: Smooths oily skin that shows large pores; heals inflammation of the skin; add to bath and facial steam bath for cleansing.

Companion planting: does well with bush and pole beans, peas, fennel, cabbage, kohlrabi, and carrots; does not do well with cucumbers.

Harvesting: Young shoots and leaves throughout summer for seasoning; harvest early (June or July) to dry for teas so that plants can grow strong again for winter.

Culinary: Fresh and dried for fish, meat, and vegetable dishes; use sage sparingly.

Medicinal: Reduces mouth and throat inflammations; relieves stomach and intestinal problems; reduces perspiration; is a stimulant; heals wounds; *do not use for a prolonged period.*

Black Elderberry
Sambucus nigra
Caprifoliaceae

Characteristics: Shrub or tree; grows up to 23ft (7m) tall; white to yellow-white flowers in June and July with intense fragrance; drooping clusters of violet-black berries.

Warning: Do not eat berries that are still green. Cook ripe berries before eating. Berries can cause nausea and vomiting unless ripe and cooked.

Active Substances: Essential oils, flavonoid, tannic acid, mucilage, glycoside, organic acids, coloring agents, vitamins A and C.

Cultivation: Sunny locations; fertile

Black elderberry in bloom.

and sufficiently moist soil; mulch and feed yearly with compost; plant in spring with specimens from a nursery that are one or two years old; every year, cut back the stems that carried the fruit.

Harvesting: Flowers in July; berries in September and October.

Culinary: Dip flowers in thin dough and fry as pancakes; fruits for juice, soup, wine, jams, and jellies; natural food coloring.

Medicinal: Flowers and hot juice promote perspiration in cases of colds accompanied by fever; acts as a diuretic and mild laxative; helps insomnia; relieves migraine headaches; soothing and cleansing.

Cosmetic: Add dried flowers to bath to smooth skin; is calming and cleansing.

Salad Burnet or Meadow Pimpernel
Sanguisorba minor
Rosaceae

Characteristics: Perennial; grows up to 24in (60cm) tall; reddish flowers with green-red petals from May to June; leaves have an aromatic, spicy taste.

Active Substances: Tannic acid, saponin, flavonoid, and vitamin C.

Cultivation: Sunny to partially shady locations; prefers light, lime-containing soil; feed every year in spring with compost; sow seeds in spring in rows 10in (25cm) apart; propagate through division; cut back vigorously in case of mildew infestation to allow new, healthy growth to resume; may remove flowers

Black elderberry with ripe berries.

Salad burnet.

to encourage better leaf development; will grow in containers.

Companion planting: does well with all perennial herbs that do not grow too vigorously and are of the same height.

Harvesting: Fresh leaves and young shoots throughout year; aroma strongest after rain.

Culinary: Leaves fresh or frozen for salads, eggs, cottage cheese, green sauce (see page 65), herbal sauces, herbal butter, vegetables, tomato dishes, fish, and meat; do not boil.

Medicinal: Tea from fresh flowers stimulates appetite; supports digestion; cleanses blood.

Cotton Lavender
Santolina chamaecyparissus
Compositae

Characteristics: Perennial; grows up to 20in (50cm) tall; porous, warm soil; in rough climates, protect during winter with straw; propagate through cuttings, runners, and division in summer; must cut back yearly or will become bare in the lower parts; also recommended as a border; will grow in containers.

Active Substances: Essential oils, flavonoid, and tannic acid.

Salad burnet in bloom.

Cotton lavender.

Cultivation: Sunny location; prefers porous, warm soil; in harsh climates, protect with straw during winter; propagate through cuttings, runners, and division; cut back yearly; will grow in containers.

Harvesting: Shoots with flowers or flowers alone in June and July; also used for dried flower arrangements and in house for fragrance; store dried in glass jars.

Medicinal: In the past, used for worms and to relieve cramps; today only used to protect against moths (dried, in small bags).

Summer Savory
Satureja hortensis
Labiatae

Characteristics: Annual; grows up to 16in (40cm) tall; white or pink-violet flowers bloom from July to September; spicy fragrance.

Winter savory (*Satureja montana*) is a perennial plant, not at all demanding as to location and similar in use to summer savory.

Active Substances: Essential oils with carvacrol, mucilage, and bitters.

Cultivation: Sunny to partially shady locations; humus-rich, slightly lime-rich soil; winter savory will grow in rock garden; water when needed; add compost before seeding; sow seeds April through July in rows 10in (25cm) apart; needs light for germination; propagate winter savory through division; both summer and winter savory will grow in containers.

Companion planting: does well with bush and pole beans, endives, fennel, lettuce, beets, and onions.

Summer savory.

Winter savory.

Harvesting: Leaves fresh daily until onset of winter; pick leaves for drying before onset of blooming; dry or freeze.

Culinary: Fresh or dried for meat, fish,

Jenny stonecrop.

game, cold cuts, legumes, potato dishes, and one-pot meals.
Medicinal: Supports digestion; relieves cramps; prevents flatulence; is an expectorant.

Jenny Stonecrop
Sedum reflexum
Crassulaceae

Characteristics: Perennial; grows up to 10in (25cm) tall; yellow flowers in July and August; fruits "explode" when wet, expelling the seeds; pleasantly sour taste.
Active Substances: Mucilage, tannic acid, and mineral salts.
Cultivation: Sunny locations; humus-rich, dry soil; propagate through division and runners; undemanding; will grow in containers.

Companion planting: does well with all plants growing in a rock garden. In the herb garden, other, more vigorously growing plants often crowd it out.

Harvesting: Tips from delicate shoots and fresh leaves throughout year, not only when plant is in bloom; only use when fresh, even during winter months.
Culinary: Spicy side dish; garnish for raw vegetables, salads, sauces, and herbal vinegar.
Medicinal: Use juice of young shoots in raw vegetable salads to cleanse blood; is a diuretic.

White Mustard
Sinapis alba
Cruciferae

Characteristics: Annual; grows up to 10in (25cm) tall; yellow, light flowers from June to September depending on when seeds went into ground; seeds are pale yellow, hot and spicy.
Active Substances: Seeds contain mustard-oil glycosides, heavy oils, and mucilage.

White mustard.

Cultivation: Sunny and partly shady locations; prefers lime-rich soil; in general, not very demanding; if sufficient compost provided before seeding, no additional feeding required; make several subsequent seedings, starting in March in rows 8in (20cm) apart; rapidly growing plant (see page 57); ideal herb to grow during winter months; will grow in containers.

> Companion planting: works well in the general garden. It is an ideal companion for all vegetables; however, try to avoid planting near cabbage.

Harvesting: Seeds early in the morning when pods are ripe; allow to dry on flat surface in sun; harvest new shoots as soon as 4in (10cm) long.

Culinary: Fresh new shoots for salads, raw vegetables, and toppings; add seeds to beet dishes; use to make your own mustard.

Medicinal: Stimulates appetite and digestion; externally, stimulates skin; *use with care.*

Comfrey
Symphytum officinale
Boraginaceae

Characteristics: Perennial: grows up to ½in (1.5cm) tall; mauve, pink, violet, and white flowers from May to August; strong root stock.

Active Substances: Mucilage, tannic acid, and alkaloids.

Cultivation: Sunny and partially shady locations; moist, fertile soil; feed yearly in spring with compost; propagate through division and root sections; plant in spring; assure at least 40in (1m) distance between each plant.

> Because the plants grow vigorously, they are not good "neighbors" for other plants; you can use the flowers and leaves to produce yellow dyes.

Comfrey.

Comfrey flowers.

Harvesting: Fresh leaves for external use; roots to dry in fall and spring.
Medicinal: Apply leaves in cases of sprains, strains, and bruises, but only for a short period of time. Use freshly mashed or dried roots for healing purposes; most well-known application is as a wrap for fractures, wounds, rheumatic joint problems, and skin inflammation.
Cosmetic: Use lotion from roots for acne and cracked skin.

Thyme
Thymus vulgaris
Labiatae

Thyme is another herb that becomes a bee pasture!
Characteristics: Miniature shrub; grows up to 16in (40cm) tall; pink to dark violet flowers from May till September; spicy aroma.

Thymus × *citriodorus*, lemon thyme, has a characteristic lemony aroma. This variety is more demanding in terms of soil and climate; needs winter protection in cold areas.

Active Substances: Essential oils with thymol, tannic acid, bitters, and flavonoid.
Cultivation: Sunny locations; lime-rich, dry soil; in general, watering not necessary (good plant for dry climates); feed with compost in spring; sow seeds in spring in rows 10in (25cm) apart; needs light for germination; propagate through division, cuttings, and runners; easy to care for; will grow in containers.

Companion planting: does well with cabbage.

Harvesting: Continuous picking of fresh, young shoots just prior to blooming to assure best possible quality.

Thyme.

Lemon thyme.

Fenugreek
Trigonella foenum-graecum
Leguminosae

Characteristics: Annual; grows up to 16in (40cm) tall; yellow-white flowers in May and June; characteristic, strong fragrance.
Active Substances: Mucilage, saponin, essential oils, and heavy oil.
Cultivation: Sunny locations; light, humus-rich soil; sow seeds starting in April in rows 10in (25cm) apart.

Companion planting: does well as interim plant between faster, stronger-growing, and taller plants. Harvest when neighboring plants need more room.

Culinary: Boil fresh or dried to use with meat, vegetables, potatoes, cottage cheese, and sauces; add lemon thyme to homemade wine and spirits; thyme is a basic ingredient of a bouquet garni (see page 65) and of many different spicy mixtures.
Medicinal: Is an expectorant; soothes coughs; relieves cramps during coughing and in case of bronchitis; excellent addition to the bath; use as a mouthwash; soothes the stomach and improves digestion; *do not use in high amounts or over a long period of time.*
Cosmetic: Use as compress or in facial steam bath; cleansing effects for blemished and oily skin; strengthens scalp when used as hair lotion.

Comfrey.

Harvesting: Seeds about four weeks after plant blooms; tie into bunches, hang upside down, and dry.

Culinary: Sometimes ground, roasted, and used as seasoning for meat dishes; one of herbs used to make curry.

Medicinal: Strengthening; used during convalescence; used with compresses for nail-bed infection; as tea for cough, boil ½oz (15g) seeds in 20oz (600ml) water.

Cosmetic: Stimulates skin, particularly after treatment for skin problems.

Nasturtium
Tropaeolum majus
Tropaeolaceae

The plant releases a cresslike, peppery aroma.

Characteristics: Annual; grows up to 12in (30cm) tall, new shoots up to 6½ft (2m); beautiful flowers in different colors from June to September; sensitive to frost; sweet aroma.

Active Substances: Rich in vitamin C.

Cultivation: Sunny locations; humusrich, light soil; needs sufficient amount of water; to prevent rapid growth, do not give additional fertilizer; sow seeds over an area or in rows 12in (30cm) apart; will grow in containers and around poles.

Companion planting: does well with peas, cucumbers, potatoes, cabbage, kohlrabi, and pole beans; does not do well with tomatoes.

Harvesting: Young shoots, leaves, and ⋯rs continuously for seasoning; use ⋯esh.

⋯**y:** Leaves, flowers, and shoots ⋯n to salads, raw vegetable sal-
⋯ings, cottage cheese, and
⋯gar; put up seeds in vinegar
⋯ent for capers; *do not use in*

Nasturtium growing on a fence.

Attractive nasturtium flowers.

large amounts; edible flowers are wonderful garnish.

Medicinal: Stimulates appetite and digestion; used in cases of infection of the bronchial and urinary tracts.

Coltsfoot leaves ready for harvesting.

Coltsfoot flowers ready for harvesting.

Coltsfoot
Tussilago farfara
Compositae

Characteristics: Perennial; grows up to 12in (30cm) tall; yellow flowers from February to April.

Active Substances: Mucilage, tannic acid, inulin, and traces of alkaloids.

Cultivation: Sunny and partially shady locations; lime-rich and sufficiently moist soil; sow seeds in spring and thin to 8in (20cm) apart; propagate through division.

Harvesting: Flowers after they open; leaves April to June.

Culinary: *According to latest findings, do not use young leaves steamed as vegetables.*

Medicinal: Apply crushed leaves externally to ulcers, various inflammations, and sprains; internally for the relief of dry coughs and inflammation of the gums and throat.

Restrict the internal use to a short period of time because scientists have found liver-damaging and cancer-causing agents in this plant.

Cosmetic: Facial lotion for blemished, oily, and inflamed skin with large pores; to help oily hair and dandruff, use a brew made from flowers.

Stinging Nettle
Urtica dioica
Urticaceae

Characteristics: Perennial; to 48in (1.2m) tall; greeni from June to October in th hemisphere.

Stinging nettle.

Valerian.

Urtica urens, a smaller, annual stinging nettle, is not grown as often.

Active Substances: Generous amounts
of chlorophyll, minerals, vitamin C,
and flavonoid in the root tips.
Cultivation: Sunny to partially shady
locations; fertile soil; seeds need relatively warm soil temperature for germination, therefore, do not seed too
early; if necessary, cover after seeding;
propagate through root division.
Harvesting: Young shoots continuously until onset of blooming for fresh
use; for tea, pick leaves several times
before plant goes into bloom; roots in
fall or spring when plants are three
years old; seeds in September and October.
Culinary: Fresh leaves to prepare as for
spinach and herbal soups; raw
(scalded) for fresh herbal condiments.
Medicinal: As tea, is a diuretic; lenses
blood; tea also used for rheumatism
and problems of urinary tract; relieves

spring tiredness; ground seeds stimulate body functions in case of exhaus-
tion.
Cosmetic: Rinsing with stinging nettle
tea strengthens hair, reduces dandruff,
and controls hair loss (*not for blonds.*)

Valerian
Valeriana officinalis
Valerianaceae

We also know valerian as common valerian and garden heliotrope. A valerian
native to America is *V. edulis*, prized for
its carrot-like root.
Characteristics: Perennial shrub;
grows 20–60in (50–150cm) tall; whitish
to pink-red flowers from June to August; pleasant fragrance; short, barrel-
shaped root stock releases strong
aroma when drying.
Active Substances: Essential oils, alkaloids, and glycosides.

Valerian roots.

Medicinal: As tea and tincture (valerian drops), calms nerves; improves sleep; helps nervous stomach, intestinal and heart problems if no contraindications are present.

Great Mullein
Verbascum thapsus
Scrophulariaceae

Particularly decorative in an herbal garden, great mullein becomes a bee pasture!

Characteristics: Biennial; grows up to 6½ft (2m) tall; yellow flowers from July to September in second year.

Active Substances: Mucilage; saponin, and flavonoid.

Cultivation: Sunny and partially shady locations; humus-rich, fertile soil; add compost to soil before planting; seed in fall or spring, spread out or plant 16 × 16in (40 × 40cm) apart; propagate through division; will grow in containers.

Companion planting: none recommended. This plant is too dominant!

Harvesting: Roots in October or early spring; wash roots and divide stock, then dry.

Great mullein.

In times past, people thought vervain possessed magical powers.

Cultivation: Sunny locations; fertile soil; seed in spring in rows, thin out to 20in (50cm) apart; self-seeding; will grow in containers.

Harvesting: Flowers continuously throughout summer; carefully spread on a flat, cloth-covered surface to dry.

Culinary: Adds beautiful color to tea; flowers add aroma to homemade liquor.

Medicinal: As tea, stimulates metabolism; is an expectorant; soothing for bronchitis, cough, and hoarseness; cleanses blood; is a diuretic.

Cosmetic: As tea, used for skin blemishes.

Vervain
Verbena officinalis
Verbenaceae

Characteristics: Perennial; grows up to 40in (1m) tall; delicate violet flowers in summer; leaves have pleasant, aromatic fragrance.

Active Substances: Glycosides, essential oils, and mucilage.

Cultivation: Sunny locations; undemanding, does well in every type of soil; add compost to soil before seeding and once more during year; benefits from mulching; propagate by division of roots or portions of older root stock in fall or spring; will grow in containers.

Harvesting: Just before blooming; store dried in glass jars or cans.

Medicinal: Stimulates metabolism; is a diuretic; relieves cramps; use to gargle when hoarse; in the past, used for different complaints, today, hardly ever used; fresh, crushed leaves applied externally said to help heal wounds.

Cosmetic: Facial lotion for oily skin.

Companion planting: does well when planted with all herbs of moderate growth.

Index

(Illustrations are referenced with boldface page numbers.)

Metric Conversion

1 in = 25.4 mm	1 mm = 0.039 in
1 ft = 30.5 cm	1 m = 3.28 ft
1 cup = 0.24 liters	1 liter = 0.42 cups
1 tsp = 5 ml	1 Tb = 15 ml
1 oz = 28 g	1 lb = 0.45 kg